Peter Wolf (Ed.)
Called – Consecrated – Sent

Peter Wolf (Editor)

Called

Consecrated

Sent

Selected Texts
of Father Joseph Kentenich
about the Priesthood

Schoenstatt Editions USA

Translated from the German by Mary Jane Hoehne, 2009

Schoenstatt Sisters of Mary
W 284 N 404 Cherry Lane
Waukesha, Wisconsin 53188
schoenstattedusa@schsrsmary.org

ISBN 1-59438-010-4
© 2009 Schoenstatt Editions USA
All rights reserved

Printed by Badger Press Inc.

My gratitude goes to all who have helped me with the translation of this book.

German title: Berufen–geweiht–gesandt

© 2009 Schoenstatt Verlag
56179 Vallendar, Germany
All rights reserved
www.schoenstatt-verlag.de
Layout and cover: Oskar Buehler
ISBN 978-3-935396-21-9

Father Joseph Kentenich
for the hundredth anniversary
of his ordination to the priesthood

Contents 7

Preface

On July 8, 2010, it will be one hundred years since Father Joseph Kentenich was ordained a priest in the house chapel of the Mission House of the Pallottines in Limburg. Many priests and lay people of his worldwide foundation will gratefully celebrate this day because they all have experienced the extraordinary fruitfulness of his priesthood. The encouraging experience of the Pauline Year which awakened vibrant life in the Schoenstatt Movement and in wide circles of the Church, gave rise to the idea of observing this jubilee in a similar manner. As in the Pauline Year, a book with texts by Joseph Kentenich is made available which, in view of the anniversary of his priestly ordination, revolves around the topic of "priesthood." Shortly before finalizing the collection of texts, we learned about the surprising and joyful announcement of Pope Benedict XVI declaring a Year of the Priest that is to run from June 19, 2009 to June 19, 2010. He connects it with the 150th anniversary of the death of the saintly "Cure of Ars." We are happy to accept the Holy Father's invitation and add testimonials from the life and work of the priest Joseph Kentenich, whose beatification process is about to be closed in the Diocese of Trier and then shortly will be continued in Rome.

In view of the one hundredth anniversary of Father Kentenich's priestly ordination, this year provides an opportunity for priests to reorient themselves by his understanding of the priestly office and to be inspired through his impulses and suggestions on how to live a life grounded in the grace of their priestly calling and the Sacrament of Priesthood. The large movement of lay men and women initiated by Father Kentenich also wants to celebrate their priestly founder and thank God for his fruitful priesthood. It illustrates how vocations could thrive around him, and how a sense of togetherness with mutual esteem and complementation developed. In these texts we also meet once more the Apostle Paul in whose school Joseph Kentenich found inspiration and enrichment.

I sincerely thank all who have assisted me in the discovery of a wide range of sources supplying the texts in which Father Kentenich, during the many years of his activity, spoke about the priesthood and a priestly life. First of all, I wish to thank my confreres Dr. Bernd Biberger, Father Oskar Buehler, and Rector Msgr. Hans Schnocks, who together with me have felt interiorly compelled to compile these texts. I am grateful to Sister M. Pia Buesge of the Schoenstatt Sisters of Mary, Dr. Gertrud Pollack of the Institute of the Ladies of Schoenstatt, Elisabeth and Bernhard Neiser as well as Marianne and Adolf Defrancesco of the Institute of Schoenstatt Families, as well as Dr. Herbert King and Dr. P. Joachim Schmiedl of the Institute of Schoenstatt Fathers, for their leads and suggestions. I also thank the general governments of the Schoenstatt Sisters of Mary and of the Schoenstatt Fathers for granting copyright permission. I am grateful to the Schoenstatt Verlag under the direction of Sister Mariéle Mierswa for undertaking the task of printing and publishing the book.

May the selected texts and the introductory comments help people outside and inside the Schoenstatt Movement to see the priesthood and its mission in a new light and to rediscover it in the thinking and life of Father Joseph Kentenich.

Mount Moriah, March 25, 2009
Dr. Peter Wolf

Introduction

Joseph Kentenich was ordained a priest on July 8, 1910, by Bishop Heinrich Vieter from Cameroon in the house chapel of the Mission House of the Pallottines at Limburg. Eight candidates were ordained that day. On July 10, 1910, he celebrated his primiz, his first holy Mass. He was assisted by the provincial, Father Michael Kolb, while Father Karl Stehr preached the sermon. The wooden crucifix given to him by his mother for this day can still be seen in the Father Kentenich House on Mount Schoenstatt. The remembrance card of his first holy Mass with the words he had chosen as a motto for his priestly ministry: "O my God, grant that all minds be united in the truth and all hearts in love" is preserved there as well. As is documented, he also celebrated a holy Mass in his home parish of Gymnich to mark his priestly ordination.

After his ordination, the newly ordained priest, Joseph Kentenich, spent the first months in Limburg and in Ehrenbreitstein. Beginning in the fall of 1911, he assumed a teaching position at the Pallottine high school of the minor seminary. From the start, he helped out on weekends in the neighboring parishes where he heard confessions and celebrated Eucharist on Sundays. He was repeatedly in

13

Hermeskeil in the Hunsrueck (a region in the middle of Rhineland-Palatinate), in Diez, Lahn, in the parish church of Limburg, in Sayn, in Rheinbrohl, and in various churches in Koblenz. His first sermons date back to this time. They demonstrate how he explained the faith to his audience and how he took up and commented on Church affairs in a contemporary language.

In September 1912, Father Kentenich was transferred to Schoenstatt and in October was appointed spiritual director of the minor seminary of the Pallottines. This responsibility gave him an opportunity to develop and give expression to his own style of priestly service. At the time, the minor seminary was undergoing a period of radical change, and his predecessors had resigned. The new spiritual director tried to reach the young students by way of trust and freedom. He awakened their own personal initiative and co-responsibility, particularly also in the area of the spiritual life; he did not primarily refer to given rules and established forms. By supporting the young people first in founding a missionary club and shortly thereafter a Marian Sodality, he provided a space where their personal initiative and freedom could unfold.

The priestly ministry of the spiritual director consisted mainly in giving talks and in countless

14

private conversations. He was interested in the young people and invested great trust in them. He listened and encouraged. He enjoyed the uniqueness and originality of each individual. Bonds and new relationships developed. The boys in his charge were generally students of the Pallottines who showed an interest in the priesthood and possibly in becoming missionaries in Africa. Father Kentenich was able to awaken in them a desire to strive in developing their own unique personalities. He motivated them to get to know themselves and to prepare themselves for their future professions through self-education and apostolic responsibility for each other. He guided them toward a Marian devotion appropriate for boys their age and he relied on Mary's educational influence, also during the war. He won them over to his favorite idea of moving the Blessed Mother to choose the old St. Michael chapel as a place of grace.

For a few years after World War I, Father Kentenich lived in Engers (near Koblenz, Germany) where he held the position of house and hospital chaplain and where he further developed existing contacts. He extended his activity and reached out to seminarians in priests' seminaries of various German dioceses. Time and again, he was invited as a speaker and retreat master. He maintained contacts, visited individuals, and emerging groups of theologians.

Reactions and responses to these talks and discussions were recorded in the periodical "Sal Terrae" founded at that time.

In maintaining a living contact with many young priests and seminarians, the Schoenstatt Work grew, and in the twenties women felt drawn to it as well. People from various professions, also from the academic world, became interested and attended conferences in Schoenstatt.

From 1929 on, Father Kentenich began to reach out even further into various circles of priests. Almost every month he offered a retreat for priests. In 1934, 2631 priests attended his retreats. Every year he developed a new theme for his retreats. During these retreats and between the talks and often far into the night, Father Kentenich made himself available for personal conversations and for the Sacrament of Confession. Repeatedly he commented that these times were more important to him than the talks themselves. His priestly guidance and counsel were sought by many, and in the thirties and forties he was probably the most popular and sought-after retreat master in Germany. Approximately one third of the German clergy attended his retreats during that time.

Yet not only priests sought and needed his spiritual guidance. During this time, in Schoenstatt the movement had also been growing. Retreat after retreat, convention after convention took place in the "Bundesheim" (Retreat House, Schoenstatt) which had opened in 1928. In the meantime, more priests from among the Pallottines and the diocesan priests joined him in serving the growing movement. In the so-called "Artusrunde,"[1] he regularly met with them for an exchange of ideas and common strategic planning.

Years of maximum engagement and untiring apostolic activity were interrupted by his imprisonment in the Gestapo prison (Secret State Police) in Koblenz with a four-week solitary confinement in total darkness. Like St. Paul, he tried to understand and use this time in order to draw his followers ever more deeply into an unreserved readiness to accept God's will (symbolized in a signed blank-check) and into the total self-surrender ("inscriptio") to God. He lived out his priesthood with a radical consistency which drew others into the world of faith and into the reality of being members of Christ according to Pauline thinking. There in prison, he wrote the "Carmel Letters"

---

[1] *"King Arthur's Knights of the Round Table" – the name given to a group of priests working closely with Father Kentenich.*

about the image of Christ, which moved and gripped him deeply. In the Adsum ("I'm ready") Prayer *penned in the Koblenz prison, Father Kentenich upgraded the Adsum of his priestly ordination by including his readiness to lay down his life.* Connecting the offering of his life with the Blessed Mother's power of intercession, he petitioned her to give his followers the grace that they might learn to live and die for Christ. Illegally and secretly, he celebrated Eucharist in his prison cell every day.

In March 1942, Father Kentenich was transported from Koblenz to the Dachau concentration camp where he remained a prisoner until April 1945. As prisoner No. 29392, he was at first interned at the admission block, then in the block of Polish priests and finally in the priests' barrack # 26. It was a time of severe tribulation and perseverance. Even in these circumstances, he did not give up living and ministering as a priest. Even in the concentration camp, he conducted retreats and for many months gave talks in the evening for the priests imprisoned with him. One of his topics was "The apocalyptic priest." From the Book of Revelation, he sought to draw consolation and strength in order to be able to bear witness to Christ throughout the imprisonment and afterwards reconquer Germany for Christ. He urged his fellow priests to live a common priestly life even in the conditions of the concentration camp. A *total of seven groups met regularly. For them Father Kentenich composed the canonical hours [of the "Schoenstatt Office"]. He did so in rhyme in order to obscure the content. Some of his confreres learned these prayers by heart in order to use them as a substitute for their breviary. In this way, they were able to continue praying their priestly breviary under these trying and harsh conditions. [Blessed] Karl Leisner expressed his gratitude for these canonical hours in a letter which has been preserved.*

On four different occasions, Father Kentenich was able to celebrate Eucharist at the altar in the chapel of Barrack 26. It is the same altar at which Karl Leisner, a member of one of the Schoenstatt groups, was ordained a priest by a French bishop in the concentration camp and shortly thereafter celebrated his first and only Mass. Today, this very altar, preserved in the Priests' House on Mount Moriah in Schoenstatt, is a place where many people are spiritually drawn into this special time of grace in Father Kentenich's life.

The very measures taken by the ruling regime in order to restrict and limit Father Kentenich and his priestly ministry accomplished the very opposite. From the hell of the Dachau concentration camp, he stayed in contact with his foundation. From there he directed and guided the Sisters' community he had founded in 1926 and virtually dictated volumes in order to cultivate their spiritual life, like "Marianische Werkzeugsfroemmigkeit" [Marian Instrument Piety], "Unterweisungen ueber das Gebet" [A guide to prayer], and the "Hirtenspiegel" [Shepherd's Mirror]. Slowly a number of "Dachau Prayers" came into existence which, soon after Father Kentenich's liberation from the concentration camp, were published under the title "Himmelwaerts" [Heavenwards]. With these prayers, the priest J. Kentenich bequeathed to his spiritual family a great treasure which serves as a school of prayer, and to this very day plays an important role in the Schoenstatt Movement. His confinement in the concentration camp led to important contacts with prisoners of other nationalities and with Protestant ministers. Open to the guidance of Divine Providence, Joseph Kentenich took risks and in the middle of the concentration camp dared to proclaim the "Schoenstatt International" and to found both the Schoenstatt Family Work and the Institute of the Schoenstatt Brothers of Mary.

Unbroken, Father Kentenich returned from his imprisonment in the concentration camp and continued his priestly activity. Motivated by an even deeper conviction of his mission, he wanted to launch his foundation into the Church, into the sciences, and into the international world. His great world trip which followed played a decisive role in introducing and establishing Schoenstatt in several Latin American countries, in Africa, and in the US.

His wish to make his foundation available to the Church and to submit it to examination was not an immediate success. Two visitations were initiated – an episcopal and a canonical visitation – which resulted in a decree separating him from his work and finally exiling him to Milwaukee, Wisconsin in the USA. This "second imprisonment" which would last fourteen years was even more trying and more painful for the priest J. Kentenich because it was imposed by the Church – the Church he loved. On the way into exile, he conducted several tertianships for confreres in the community of the Pallottines. These courses – some of which lasted four weeks – contain an abundance of life experiences which the priest Joseph Kentenich passed on to his fellow priests. Generations of priests will draw from these riches.

In 1959, Father Kentenich accepted the responsibility to minister to the German community in St. Michael's Church in Milwaukee. He was entirely dedicated to this task. The people in this parish community were completely unaware of his

21

foundation that spanned the globe. For them he was simply their pastor. Since the majority of the members of this parish were refugees from Eastern Europe, he tried to give them a sense of belonging and make them feel at home in the faith and in the Church. Many looked to him for counsel and help in all types of worries and problems. They felt accepted and understood. He was like a father to them.

Together with confreres of my priests' community, I have repeatedly visited Milwaukee during the last years, and I have met people who had known Father Kentenich. To this day they speak with deep gratitude about "their father." For many it had been a great sorrow when, after fourteen years, he was called back to Rome and his exile ended. In a conversation with Father Kentenich, Cardinal Bea commented on the end of this exile, "Without the Council you would never have been understood." In an audience on December 22, 1965, the Holy Father Pope Paul VI confirmed his rehabilitation; that is, his restoration to his previous position in the Schoenstatt Work. On that occasion, the founder assured the Holy Father that, "together with his Family, he would make every effort to actualize the post-conciliar mission of the Church as perfectly as possible."

He had three more years in Schoenstatt, Germany. These were years marked by a post-conciliar spirit of optimism. These were years marked by the joy of being reunited [with the Schoenstatt Family] and of being reassured that his work had a mission for the Church. These were years marked by the completion and the rounding out of the founding phase of his communities. The number of encounters and talks, of retreats and conferences is virtually immeasurable.

On September 15, 1968, the Feast of the Seven Sorrows of Mary, the sisters of a whole province were looking forward to celebrating Eucharist with him in the newly built Church of the Blessed Trinity and to meeting with him afterwards. It would be the last holy Mass of his priestly life. After his private thanksgiving in the sacristy, he collapsed and died lying on the floor. The hours and days following his death were one great sign manifesting the fruitfulness of his priesthood. Day and night, people kept coming and passing by his open casket where he lay vested in a white vestment. They wished to express that they owed an immense debt of gratitude to this priest and that they were committed to pass on his message and his love for the Church.

Dr. Peter Wolf

The Expectations a Priest Faces

Then came my appointment
as spiritual director
– entirely without my doing.
Hence it must be God's will.
I am resigned to it,
and I am determined to fulfill my duties
to each and every one of you
as perfectly as possible.
I now place myself completely
at your disposal
with all that I am and have:
my knowledge and ignorance,
my ability and inability,
but above all, my heart.

Joseph Kentenich, October 27, 1912

He who is and wants to become a priest, faces many different types of challenges. This reality is not new. In a sermon Father Kentenich preached on the occasion of a newly ordained priest's first holy Mass, he invited his audience to clearly see the often contradictory expectations people have of a priest. On the one hand, there is the person of the saintly Cure of Ars, who above all represents a priesthood completely oriented to the supernatural. Other people prefer a priest who is more accomplished in dealing with the world. Again others consider it important that a priest be more people-oriented, casual and personable. Father Kentenich was adept at taking up these contradictory expectations and uniting them in a healthy and fruitful balance.

In his retreats, he wanted to make his confreres realize the challenges they face due to the powerful dynamics of the times, and he guided them in interpreting these challenges and consciously confronting them. In this way, he helped them to be alert and open to the signs of the times; he encouraged them to be involved and committed and to let nothing dampen their spirits, but to go forward and look with confidence into the future regarding the Church on the new shore.

In his retreats, he talked about the tension which arises from the priestly ideal of self-giving, on the one hand, and the need for each priest to preserve his own identity, on the other. In talks and personal conversations, he helped many priests use this tension constructively instead of skirting around it. This very tension also makes it necessary that, with all his personal involvement and his commitments, a priest cares for himself and his health and that he takes quality time for his own spiritual life.

Confronted with Contradictory Expectations

From: J. Kentenich, Sermon at a newly ordained priest's first holy Mass with the German community at St. Michael's Church, Milwaukee, February 7, 1965

What do people expect of a priest today? This question leads us to the various ideals which are suggested to us time and time again. At least they express our longing. Whether or not we have made them our own is another question. Thinking of a priest, of a Catholic priest, what is the world's longing today? I wonder whether this longing is not essentially identical with the secret longing in our own hearts. On the one hand, we see priests who are revered, who bear the characteristic, the indelible mark on their forehead: distinctly supernatural, otherworldly priests. Our time has a tremendous need for them, a need for priests who are firmly grounded in the supernatural reality.

When we hear, for example, how important a person like the Cure of Ars is for people today, then we know what is meant. [People want] men, priests who are completely at home with God and in some sense personify a type of priest who flees from this world. A secret longing! A priest is often called *homo Dei*, a man of God; that is, a man who is completely grounded in God – even today when people flee from God; a man who sides with God and considers it his task and mission to announce the interests of the eternal God everywhere today – not only by way of words but, above all, by his whole being, by his whole personal conduct, by his virtuous life and example.

A second type of priest who also stirs a great deal of interest today, in some way seems to represent the opposite. He is not the priest who actually flees from the world and seeks God passionately; he is the urbane priest who is adept at dealing with the world yet without allowing the features of the eternal God to be erased from his face, from his whole person. Where this desire is expressed, we also have to take for granted that it indicates a problem which the modern person does not know how to solve. We have been thrown and tossed into modern life, and we must face it: On the one hand, we should enjoy what cultural life has to offer; we should accept, joyfully accept what the world has to offer today, and on the other hand, we should also be wholly God's own. It is very difficult to combine this world and the next; it is very difficult to surrender ourselves entirely to Almighty God and yet be firmly grounded in today's modern life.

A third type of priest; I'll shortly add a fourth. At issue are priests who are close to the people, priests we would like to call "folksy priests,"or taking an expression from contemporary literature: *"Schnapspriester."*[2] A rather strange and somewhat risky expression.

---

[2] *Schnapspriester*, literally whiskey priests; that is, vulnerable and weak priests

To put it drastically: " folksy priests." These are priests who come from among the people, priests who interiorly experience people's problems, especially their social problems, problems arising from particular social strata; priests who see their task in helping to overcome these problems.

"Schnapspriester." Well, this is a strange ideal which can often be noticed on the horizon and is used especially in literature and by the movie industry in ever new ways: Priests who themselves are vulnerable, weak and helpless – *"Schnapspriester."* Hence this refers to a type of priest who himself has succumbed to the passions of modern life, of the modern person, yet keeps reaching for the heights in order to be redeemed by Christ and, in turn, channel redemptive grace to others.

Why am I saying all this? I wonder whether we understand each other. It should motivate us to listen attentively: What kind of priestly ideal do we carry in our hearts?

Challenged by the Dynamics of the Times

From: J. Kentenich. Die moderne priesterliche Werktagsheiligkeit, Retreat for priests, Schoenstatt 1939 [Everyday sanctity for the modern priest]

Our times are particularly marked by absolute dynamics. If I want to carry out my priestly ministry in today's world, I myself will have to remain flexible or I will be tossed aside. I must have an ear and listen, I must understand. We will not accomplish a great deal with theology alone, without the help of psychology and pedagogy. Our modern time can be compared to youngsters in their teens. How difficult it is to educate boys and girls in their teens.

What should we do? First, remain calm and rest in ultimate universal principles; second, understand that people today are extremely fickle and insecure; therefore, motivate them, don't judge and condemn so quickly. Wait and see; don't forget what we call moderate anthropological optimism. I believe in the good in others. We differentiate between three levels: the person acting on instincts, the person endowed with an intellect, and the child of God. How much conflict arises from this combination!

Look at the modern person's flight from God. Look at the modern person's coldness toward God.

Look at the modern person's suffering because of God. We have to search and ask: What can we do in order to become all things to all people?

First above all, we have to become transparencies of God. Above all, we have to strive to embody Christ in our lives. This is probably the best means to show people the way to God. We priests will always be the cause of inner unrest [reminding people of God], but in order to make this unrest a wholesome unrest, we must see to it that we ourselves have a passion for God. Constant dripping wears away the stone.

Second, our entire mode of preaching must become more positive.

Third, it takes a great deal of prayer and sacrifice. Could we do more? We should at least also try to make the Blessed Mother the patroness of those in our charge. How many dioceses in France and Belgium have consecrated themselves to the Blessed Mother. We do so with the deep conviction: What I cannot do, she must do; she is the great missionary, she will work miracles. As St. Vincent Pallotti said: *"Mater habebit curam"* (Mother will take care).

Balancing Dedication to Others and Preserving his Own Identity

From: J. Kentenich, Die moderne priesterliche Werktagsheiligkeit, Retreat for priests, Schoenstatt 1939 [Everyday sanctity for the modern priest]

Dedication to others is rooted in the nature of priesthood. The priest is fully absorbed by the Person of Christ, by his task. This unity is so deep that we may say: The ideal image of a priest portrays him as belonging to Christ ontologically and functionally. My interests vanish completely behind the interests of God. The Lord accepts us and our whole life so that we will belong to the people in the spirit of Christ. In this light we understand why we renounce marriage. We want to belong totally to Christ, and in Christ to immortal souls. What does this total belonging involve? We should speak with St. Paul: "To become all things to all people" (cf. 1 Cor 9:22). What then belongs to Christ and souls? Everything.

First, my economic possessions. Suddenly, there is a new reason for poverty. Poverty is grounded in our surrender to Christ but also in our belonging to the people. Poverty also has an apostolic dimension. God has given me my possessions so that I can give generously in order to gain influence, in order to have the possibility to practice true love. Poverty and being God's very own belong together. Their purpose is to prevent me from belonging to myself and instead to belong to the people, to belong to God.

Second, my physical strength. I should consume my strength for the salvation of souls. One cannot say anything more beautiful of a priest. Soldiers make the ultimate sacrifice for their country; a captain sinks with his ship. That's the essence of their greatness.

Third, my spiritual strength. My spiritual abilities, my mind, heart, and will belong to God and to immortal souls. I study even if I do not feel like it; I can warm up my heart and feel for the problems of those entrusted to me even if I am tired.

To whom should I give everything? I should become all things to all people. That is the reason why I forego marriage. Otherwise there is great danger that my power of love becomes stunted, enslaved. True virginity consists in [becoming all things to all people]. I have no time for other additional occupations. I devote my caring and loving service to those who are healthy, sick, marginalized, etc. I strive to be absolutely generous in my dedication to others, of going the extra mile for others, of being unstinting in my ministry. Some priests take a vow of absolute service.

Preserving my own identity! I must also care for myself. What must I safeguard? My health. Otherwise I cannot serve others. I must safeguard my holiness, and therefore I must protect my self-identity. I need quality time with God, I need time when I can enjoy being alone with God, for example in meditation. I must also preserve my priestly purity. When I constantly give myself to others, the danger is great that I lose myself, that I relate so much to others that I forget to relate to God. Tension! This twofold polarity creates tension. The first area of tension arises from giving myself. The second from preserving myself.

The first field of tension arises from giving of self. Tension arises from giving of self: a) because my giving of self is misused; b) because it is diverted. Tension arises from self-giving because it is misused.

The misuse can apply to my economic giving of self and my personal giving of self. My economic giving of self can be misused. I can give alms. I want to be absolutely poor. How easily this can be misused. How quickly people might come who do not need my help, my money. How do I solve this tension? First, what I give to the poor, I give to Christ. (See *Everyday Sanctity*). Second, it is definitely true that we have to exercise some prudence. This will lessen the tension, but not resolve it.

My personal giving of self can also be misused. I give my heart away, my caring and concern, my personal self. The misuse consists in someone's effort to connect with me on a personal level so that I might bond with that person. In order to lessen the danger to some degree, it is important for us to occupy ourselves again and again with the universalism of our apostolate, with the essence of our priestly ordination. Secondly, we must be mindful of the great principle of intactness. This means for us priests to be interiorly unselfconscious, exteriorly completely intact. Thirdly, to be devoted to the atmosphere of our family, to intensify it. If our family as a whole has a certain lifestyle, we will grow. If we understand how to dedicate ourselves and to observe moderation, we will contribute to creating this type of atmosphere in the whole family. Tension is necessary in our life or we stop making progress.

The Priest – a Man of God and a Builder of Bridges

O my God,
grant that all minds be united
in the truth and
all hearts in love.

Joseph Kentenich's remembrance card
of his first holy Mass, July 8, 1910

The challenges of the times need to be addressed. The key lies in our profound awareness of being called, in our profound consciousness of having a mission. Father Kentenich encouraged priests again and again to keep the story of their own priestly vocation alive, to take it seriously as a personal calling and the source of a healthy mission consciousness. Especially in times when religion and Christianity threaten to evaporate and fade away more and more, it is crucial that with their ministry and their existence, priests are totally committed to God and keep their focus on God. Their task of being "bridge builders" becomes increasingly relevant, the more the modern, earth-oriented person loses sight of the other shore; that is, the world of God, or seems to lose all awareness of its existence.

People's longing to experience the priest as a trustworthy witness, in fact as a "man of God," will only find an answer if priests themselves live out of a deep consciousness that they have been called and that they have a mission to fulfill.

Called by God – Consecrated to God – Sent by God

From: J. Kentenich, Introductory talk of the retreat for the Bethlehem Fathers, Immensee, Switzerland, August 9, 1937 [Childlikeness before God, p. 4 ff. Trs. by Fr. Jonathan Niehaus]

When I see my life in connection with God, I know that I am called by God, dedicated to God, sent by God.

1. Called by God

I keep in mind the dark background of our times and say to myself: The God who is so little appreciated by the modern world has called me.

In this context it may be worthwhile to recall the story of my personal priestly vocation. God called me. Deo gratias! Thanks be to God! I want to tell myself this when my vocation means difficulties for me, when on occasion I must endure bitter disappointments. I did not call myself; God called me! It was not some random third party that called me; no, my vocation comes from God! Deo gratias! Thanks be to God! Then burdensome difficulties can come my way – the God who called me will always be with me. Did not our Lord, in the prime of his life, say something similar: "The One who sent me never abandons me, for I always do what pleases him" (Jn 8:29).

In short, I ask you to return to your own vocation story and let it sink in again. This should stir the interior life of your soul. In this way the soul should become more receptive to the seeds of God's grace.

As you look back on the story of your life, I think three claims can serve as a general outline. Even though each of our vocations may have gone through very different stages of development, these three features always apply: my call is extraordinary, easily recognizable, and effective.

An extraordinary call

What do I mean by that? The call which we heard – "Come, follow me!" (Mt 19:21) – was a call which elevated us from life's ordinary planes. The word "extraordinary" is meant here in contrast to the call which ordinary Christians hear. They, too, are called by God to follow him. But relatively few are called by God to become his closest followers – to become priests!

It is an extraordinary vocation. *"Non vos me elegistis: sed ego elegi vos."* "It is not you who have chosen me, but I who have chosen you" (Jn 15:16). For the moment we only want to savor more deeply the word "God" against the background of our life. How soothing its effect! How encouraging and victorious it resounds as it penetrates our souls!

Our call was also easily recognizable, at least sooner or later. How quickly we could grasp: It was really God! Our souls may have been enfolded here and there by darkness and night, but when it really mattered, we knew it clearly.

An effective calling.

Our calling was effective. Here we can recall all the obstacles to our vocation which had to be overcome before we stood at the altar and were taken into the community as full members to do our share for God's Kingdom. I am therefore here as one called by God.

2. Dedicated to God

God has called to me: "You are mine!" God wanted that I give myself to him. I responded to God's "You are mine!" with "Here I am! I want to be yours for time and eternity!" This is another point where it would be worthwhile to review my life from the moment of my "yes" to God. I gave myself to him – privately perhaps even since childhood. Recall the moment when you first said, "Yes, I want to belong to you; nothing else matters!" Even if no one else in my family had a religious vocation, I felt and was convinced: God's plan for me is special.

I think of my private consecration, my private surrender to God. Recall what you experienced when you received the tonsure, when you were ordained a subdeacon, when you were ordained a priest. In short, relive your whole life from the standpoint: Called by God, dedicated to God!

As you recall your life's story, pause for a moment and ask yourself what you did at the time. Was it not something exceedingly rare, something exceedingly great, something that made you extremely happy and fruitful! Ponder these four words in your meditation. – My decision, my surrender to God, my consecration to God . . .

3. Sent by God

We are not only called by and dedicated to God, but also sent by God. Why did God call me? Why did I dedicate myself to him? In order to be sent by him! I received this commission at ordination. I shall receive this commission again at the end of the retreat. "As the Father has sent me, so I send you" (Jn 20:21). We did not enter the community in order to lead a quiet life on a quiet island. No, we have been drawn into the great current of the mission of the God-Man. How does that sound to someone familiar with the times around us, to those of you familiar with the pagan nations of the old variety, and who know how night and darkness are constantly engaged in battle with the light. Yes, we have been drawn into the current of the mission of the God-Man. Deo gratias! Thanks be to God! God wants his name to be glorified through us wherever he sends us.

Can we hear whether the words which applied in his day to St. Paul, also apply to us: "I will show him what great things he must suffer for my name's sake" (Acts 9:16)? To be drawn into the current of the mission of the God-Man means, of course, to also be drawn into the current of his suffering.

To be drawn into the current of his mission also means to be drawn into the great current of his work. Read in Sacred Scripture what an obligation this mission meant for the Apostles. They could not sit idly by. They had to work! The various expressions used to describe the office of the apostles expressly point this out: soldier of Christ (2 Tim 2:3), laborer in the Lord's vineyard (Mt 20:1-16), fisher of men (Mt 4:19; Mk 1:17). . . . If we are sent out we must work in earnest for immortal souls, even when it may mean our ruin. We may not seek ourselves.

All in all, please understand well these words of introduction! We do not wish to say anything great or new tonight. Our sole desire is to plunge once more into the infinite ocean of God. The eternal and infinite God envelops my life, my personal life in this extraordinarily profound manner. He has personally called me, called me by name. I could personally dedicate myself to him. He has personally sent me. I can now restudy in detail: What does my unique mission look like in the context of the work which God's providence has foreseen for me? The main thing tonight is that we draw nearer to God again – the eternal God, the infinite God, the God who is so persecuted today. To this God, who so intimately circles

45

our life, who so envelops us with his love, we want to give all glory during these days, we want to learn to glorify him anew in a heroic manner, both through our being and through our actions.

Chosen from Among the People – for the People

From: J. Kentenich, Sermon on the occasion of a newly ordained priest's first Mass with the German community at St. Michael's Church, November 3, 1963

As we often do and are used to doing, we want to go into the school of the apostle Paul for a moment. We want to process interiorly what he has to say about the mission of a Catholic priest in general. Above all, we want to try to apply it to our time, the time in which we live – a time of confusion, a time without peace, a time that is fleeing from God.

What does St. Paul tell us? In his typical way, he recapitulates everything that can be said about a priest's mission in one single sentence. I'll say it in Latin first and translate the main points of it. *Omnis pontifex ex hominibus assumptus pro hominibus constituitur in eis, quae sunt ad Deum* (Heb 5:1). In plain English it means: The priest is taken from among the people; that is to say, not from among the angels and, therefore, he does not have to be an angel. Taken from among the people; that is to say, not from among the canonized saints or saintly persons who could be canonized. Chosen from among the people! What is his task? He should educate the people – not just one or the other person but all people without exception – and lead them to a deeper understanding of their fundamental relationship with the living God in order that they will interiorly affirm this relationship and live it out in everyday life. Put differently, he should move all people without exception – speaking with our Lord – to love God with all their hearts, with all their souls, with all their minds, and with all their strength" (cf. Mk 12:30); all people – not just one or the other person, not just this or that Catholic. We might not even realize what is hidden in each of these words. I think we should take the time to dwell on and weigh every word.

First we hear the word "priest." It refers to a priest in general. For us at this very moment, the word "priest" also refers to the priest we see at the altar for the first time. Strangely enough, in this case St. Paul translates the word priest with an unusual expression: *pontifex*. What is a *pontifex*? The word indicates at the same time the special character of the priestly mission. *Pontifex* is a bridge builder.

What, then, is a priest's task? To build bridges. How can we picture the two shores being linked and connected by a bridge? On the one side, there is the living God and, on the other, the human person. The priest's task consists in connecting God and the human person in an inseparable, tender, loving, permanent union. Actually, this is nothing new; it is an old truism.

And yet, when we view this truth within the framework of today's general confusion, we realize that we live in a world that flees from God. The world around us – we think of our co-workers, of TV programs – the world is running away from God. And God himself? The words of a modern philosopher (Friedrich Wilhelm Nietzsche) are written with massive strokes into the features of our time: We have murdered the living God! Where can he still be found? Where does he still exist?

And now we are told: A priest's task in times like ours consists in changing the person who is running away from God into a person who is "addicted" to God; in letting people experience the murdered God as the living God and making him the object of an ardent, tender love. *Pontifex.*

St. Paul is quite skilled in playing with expressions. Because at issue is an important function, an extraordinary mission, he plays with expressions. He calls the priest a servant of Christ, a servant of God, a servant of the people. He calls the priest the mediator between God and humanity. At least theoretically, we know what is meant: mediator between God and humanity. The priest stands between the eternal God and humanity.

What, then, should he do? He should communicate to us humans the wisdom of God, the truth of the living God. What should he do? He should bring to us humans the mercies of God, the mysteries of the living God as they are symbolically present in the sacraments. On the other hand, he should present the wishes of the people, the needs of the people, the sins of the people, the joys of the people, the sufferings of the people to an all-loving God.

Do you understand what all this means? *Homo Dei,* a man of God – this is who a priest is. His great mission is to reunite and reconnect everything with the living God. This has been his great task in life at all times, but it is an extremely important if extremely difficult task today.

What does all this mean? When we hear the expression mediator, we automatically remember that we as Christians ultimately know only one mediator. Who is this? Christ. Through priestly ordination, the priest himself becomes a mediator in Christ in as far as he indeed deserves the name mediator; through priestly ordination, he is drawn into the character of the eternal High Priest, Jesus Christ. We have only one priest in Christianity (cf. Heb 22:24), only one mediator (cf. 1 Tim 2:5). The priest is drawn into the being and function of this one mediator. Consequently, when a priest preaches, he lends his tongue to Christ. Christ speaks through the priest. We know that when a newly ordained priest administers the sacraments or when he speaks the words of Consecration, he lends his tongue and his hands to the eternal High Priest.

In this connection, St. Paul would repeat the words: It is no longer I who speak; Christ speaks in me as a priest. It is no longer I who act as a priest when I administer the sacraments; Christ acts in me. That's why it is justified to say: A priest is a priest by God's favor, not the people's; true, he is so in order to serve the people – but by God's grace. It is God who chooses the priest and draws him into his own being, into his own priestly being and priestly ministry.

This is the meaning of our Lord's powerful words: "You did not choose me, but I chose you and appointed you that you should go and bear fruit and that your fruit should abide" (Jn 15:16). And again: "As the Father has sent me, even so I send you" (Jn 20:21).

Lastly, then, a priest's mission is ultimately founded in the Father God, in and through Christ. The priest is drawn into a mission current. The priest must continue our Lord's mission until the end of time.

Participation in the Priesthood of Christ

*There is no priesthood
but the priesthood in Christ Jesus.*

Joseph Kentenich 1939

The following texts reveal Joseph Kentenich's profound understanding of the essence of priesthood. Like the decree on the priesthood issued by Vatican II, he was radical in his acknowledgment of the biblical view that there is only one mediator between God and humanity and that all priesthood is simply a participation in the one priesthood of Jesus Christ. Father Kentenich stated this view in the language and thinking of scholastic theology of his day and consistently proclaimed it. It is worthwhile to pursue this line of thinking because, in essence, it concurs with the conciliar image of priesthood.

In his retreats, Joseph Kentenich did not limit himself to the theology of priesthood but systematically translated it into a spirituality for priests lived in everyday life. In his approach, he did not consider himself a scholar and theologian but a "liaison officer," a link between theology and life. From this orientation to theology and the conscious process of translating it into life, there emerged a specific, original priestly spirituality which has inspired many priests then and now.

Christi – the One Priest

From: J. Kentenich, Die moderne priesterliche Werktagsheiligkeit, Retreat for priests, Schoenstatt 1939 [Everyday sanctity for the modern priest]

First, ontologically seen, Christ does not stand exclusively on God's side nor exclusively on ours. He is both God and Man. Ontologically seen, he stands in the middle.

Second, he stands both on God's side and on ours.

Third, he unites, he balances seemingly irreconcilable contradictions in a wonderful harmony: the eternal God and small, insignificant creatures. The *"unio hypostatica"* is, if you wish, his priestly ordination. The moment of his incarnation is the moment of his priestly ordination. The priest's greatness consists in his being perfectly drawn into the *"unio hypostatica"* of the God-Man. In awe and reverence, we stand before the greatness of our priesthood.

Functionally, too, Christ is the only priest. He is the mediator. The definition of a priest is being a mediator; that is to say, he stands in the middle between two partners. We receive all gifts from God through Christ. What are these gifts? He brings light, life, and grace to us from God. What does he take to God from us? Through the union of his divine Person with his human nature, he offers infinite honor and glory to the eternal God.

The human priesthood originates in our Lord and remains in our Lord. Our Lord is the only priest. My priestly ministry is our Lord's ministry. It is a dual unity: Christ the human priest [and] Christ the priest who is God-Man. I'll indicate how to prove it. I'll prove that our Lord is the only priest in the present world order.

Examine St. Paul. He says: "For there is one God, and there is one mediator" (cf. 1 Tim 2:5). Read the passages on your own. In order to prevent obscuring the uniqueness of Christ's priesthood, the first priests were not called priests but elders. The only functional, ministerial priest is Christ. God demanded infinite glory. Who alone was able to offer this? Only he who combines both the divine and the human natures.

What, then is the answer to the question: What is my priesthood? A preliminary answer: It is a perfect, mysterious ontological and functional participation in the high priesthood of Christ.

Fruitful Participation in the Priesthood of Christ

From: J. Kentenich, Marianische Werkzeugsfroemmigkeit, Dachau, April-June 1944. [Marian Instrument Piety, trs. by Fr. William Brell, rev.]

Every priesthood in the Church is a participation in Christ's priesthood. It is he, therefore, who in holy unity with the human priest, whom he has drawn into his priesthood, walks through, touches, and works in our modern times. Priests are the instruments through which he teaches, guides, and sanctifies the world. He does this in an imperfect manner through those who are baptized and confirmed; in a perfect manner through the ordained priesthood by means of which he wishes to perpetuate and exercise in the world his office of teacher, priest, and shepherd until the end of times. Since the Ascension, therefore, he does not leave the world for which he died, to itself, nor is he content to be active for us in heaven as "a Lamb that had been slain" (Rev 5:6). In his priests, his transparencies, he walks constantly through the world, leading it to the Father. The indelible mark sets its bearers apart from the "world" and hands them over to Christ, the High Priest, and to his work of redemption. It implies that the chosen ones are mysteriously united to Christ as priest; it makes them "slaves" of Christ, and in and with Christ "slaves" of immortal souls.

For this reason, the apostle Paul considers himself a "slave" of Christ. He feels responsible for all, for Greeks, for Gentiles, and for Jews; he would like to become "all things to all people" in order to lead all to Christ. Christ is to take form in all, and all should "grow into the full stature of Christ." St. Paul has become the Apostle, the image of the Good Shepherd who "knows his own" and "gives his life for them"; who searches out "the sheep which do not belong to the fold." He is the Apostle to the Gentiles, an overpowering example for all who wish to sanctify and give wings to their fruitfulness in the apostolate, whether they belong to the ordained or to the lay priesthood. Christ, the eternal High Priest, and his instruments are ontologically so mysteriously interconnected and intertwined, so interdependent that one without the other cannot accomplish the task. In spite of his omnipotence, Christ does not want to sanctify the world without the free cooperation of his priests. And the priest, being only Christ's instrument, can do nothing in the order of salvation without him.

In his parable of the vine, our Lord calls attention to this: "Abide in me as I abide in you. Just as the branch cannot bear fruit by itself unless it abides in the vine, neither can you unless you abide in me. I am the vine, you are the branches. Those who abide in me and I in them bear much fruit, because apart from me you can do nothing. Whoever does not abide in me is thrown away like a branch and withers; such branches are gathered, thrown into the fire, and burned. If you abide in me, and my words abide in you, ask for whatever you wish, and it will be done for you" (Jn 15:4-7).

In his Encyclical on the Mystical Body of Jesus Christ, the Holy Father (Pope Pius XII) aptly called attention to the mutual necessity and dependence which is often not sufficiently recognized. He wrote:

"Because Christ the Head holds such an eminent position, one must not think that he does not require the help of the Body. What Paul said of the human organism is to be applied likewise to the Mystical Body: 'The head cannot say to the feet: I have no need of you' (1 Cor 12:21). It is manifestly clear that the faithful need the help of the Divine Redeemer, for He has said: 'Without me you can do nothing' (Jn 15:5), and according to the teaching of the Apostle every advance of this Mystical Body toward its perfection derives from Christ the Head (cf. Eph 4:16; Col 2:19).

Yet this, also, must be held, marvelous though it may seem: Christ has need of His members. First, because the person of Jesus Christ is represented by the Supreme Pontiff, who in turn must call on others to share much of his solicitude lest he be overwhelmed by the burden of his pastoral office, and must be helped daily by the prayers of the Church.

Moreover as our Savior does not rule the Church directly in a visible manner, He wills to be helped by the members of His Body in carrying out the work of redemption. That is not because He is indigent and weak, but rather because He has so willed it for the greater glory of His spotless Spouse. Dying on the

Cross He left to his Church the immense treasury of the Redemption, toward which she contributed nothing. But when those graces come to be distributed, not only does He share this work of sanctification with His Church, but He wills that in some way it be due to her action. This is a deep mystery, and an inexhaustible subject of meditation, that the salvation of many depends on the prayers and voluntary penance which the members of the Mystical Body of Jesus Christ offer for this intention and on the cooperation of pastors of souls and of the faithful, especially of fathers and mothers of families, a cooperation which they must offer to our Divine Savior as though they were His associates" (Pius XII, Encyclical *Mystici corporis* 44).

We are quite convinced of our dependence on Christ in the work of salvation, less so, however, of his dependence on us. If this also penetrates into our consciousness, we will understand the Lord's words from the cross: "I thirst!" (Jn 19:28), and we will answer them with a consuming zeal for souls, with a heroic striving for rich and varied fruitfulness.

No one of us intends not to bear fruit, including – actually least of all – the virginal soul. The booklet of aphorisms "The Jewel of Purity" (Fr. J. Kentenich) states very clearly how virginity and fruitfulness are interconnected. I limit myself to mentioning some of the forms of its fruitfulness.

The virginal soul forgoes marriage and the happiness connected with it not because of fear of sacrifice but to be able to fulfill the greatest commandment as perfectly as possible: "You shall love the Lord your God with your whole heart, with your whole soul, and with all your mind. This is the greatest and first commandment" (Mt 22:37). Instead of natural complementation, the virginal soul wants to realize the words of St. Paul: "The unmarried man is anxious about the affairs of the Lord, how to please the Lord; but the married man is anxious about the affairs of the world, how to please his wife, and his interests are divided" (1 Cor 7:32-33). With great sacrificial spirit, virginity is dedicated in a holy *matrimonium spirituale* (spiritual marriage) with Christ to begetting and educating spiritual children. It foregoes physical descendants in order to become all the more fruitful for the Kingdom of God by a heroic cultivation of the corporal and spiritual works of mercy. How cold, empty, and helpless the world would be without virginal souls and their activity! Countless marriages also owe their courage and strength to remain faithful to their marital vows, to master their passionate drives in a God-willed way and consequently their physical fruitfulness to the radiant and captivating continence of virginal souls. Who could possibly count all the children who owe their existence to parents thus strengthened and purified.

Original Priestly Striving for Holiness

From: J. Kentenich, Die moderne priesterliche Werktagsheiligkeit, Retreat for priests, Schoenstatt 1939 [Everyday sanctity for the modern priest]

First, my priestly piety must be Christ-centered. Through my ontological union with Christ, I have been mysteriously drawn into Christ. This defines my Christ-centered piety. A few suggestions for practical life: What can I do in order to become more Christ-centered?

(1) I have to get to know our Lord better and find joy in reading the Scriptures. If I have been grafted onto him, this is taken for granted.

(2) Learn to love our Lord more deeply. Where should this love be most ardent? In the celebration of holy Mass and in adoration of the Eucharist. During, before, and after celebrating holy Mass, commune with him in private, just the two of you. After celebrating Mass, we should hear the words: "Simon, do you love me?" Our sense of reality does not end with ideas. We also want to love our Lord personally. That's why I long to be with him before the tabernacle during the day. Just as the Apostles went to our Lord with all kinds of little things, so do we. We want to love him with all our heart. Our deep veneration of the humanity of Jesus draws us to the tabernacle because we know that through priestly

ordination our connectedness with the human nature of the God-Man is incredibly deep.

Second, my priestly piety must be Trinitarian. I am one with Christ in a union that is work-oriented as well as goal-oriented. The goal of Christ's work was the glorification of the Triune God. Nothing can perturb us. My holiness must be Trinitarian. All and everything we have done in the course of the past years leads us to the Most Holy Trinity.

Third, my priestly piety must be liturgical. Being united with Christ in a common task demands a liturgical ministry of us. We must be liturgical-minded. For a true priest this is taken for granted. Liturgical, but not falling victim to liturgicism. Let us deepen our liturgical attitude. Make use of little things. On waking up in the morning, we renew our awareness of being baptized when we make the sign of the cross. Little things often indicate greatness.

Fourth, my priestly piety must be apostolic. We form a communion of grace with Christ. The grace of priesthood is an apostolic grace for the salvation of other people as well as my own.

Fifth, my priestly piety must be Marian. In the language of St. Augustine, we are *matres Christi. "Audemus nos dicere matres Christi."* – We have the audacity to call ourselves mothers of Christ. Since we have the same nature as Mary, we have the same task, the same grace.

What is the source of a priest's Marian attitude? The titles I have just mentioned. I am only speaking as a theologian. A priest is Marian because of his union of being, work, and grace with Christ.

He is Marian because of his ontological union with Christ. The ontological union with Christ is directly rooted in the *character sacerdotalis* (priestly character). What does it give me? My priestly personality is for the human nature of the God-Man what this human nature is for the *Verbum Divinum* (Divine Word). Hence I am drawn into the humanity of Christ. Mary is the mother of the human nature of the God-Man. Therefore, she is also my mother simply because of the ontological union with Christ. She is the mother of all humanity, but especially of priests. Who is more deeply drawn into Christ than a priest? Therefore, the Blessed Mother must be the mother of priests in a singular manner.

Hence, I have to love the Blessed Mother. I have to love the Blessed Mother with an extraordinarily great childlike love. I have the courage to acknowledge that I am Marian. The family has the courage to acknowledge the Blessed Mother. [We are] Marian because we form a union of cooperation with Christ. In his encyclical on the priesthood, Pius XI said: "A priest must have a childlike love for the Blessed Mother." What reason did he give? His reason is relevant here: "Because of his union of tasks with Christ." *Similis simili gaudet* – "Birds of a feather flock together." – "Like rejoices in like." The union of cooperation with Christ is a union of goals, of tasks, and of grace. A union of goals with Christ. How helpless our Lord was during his earthly life. What did the Blessed Mother do? She was the handmaid of the Lord. A union of tasks.

A Profoundly Prophetic Task

In times of radical change,
a priest must be a prophet

Joseph Kentenich 1930

In 1940, Father Kentenich conducted a retreat for priests on the book of Revelation, entitled. "The apocalyptic priest." During the years of National Socialism with its turmoil, its hostility against the Church, and the war situation, he wanted to ground his confreres firmly in the spirit of the authentic Revelation of Christ, according to St. John. In this retreat he encouraged his audience to overcome the "type of a self-complacent or even shallow" priest and to strive for the ideal of becoming a "type of prophetic priest." He described the ideal as a prophetic priest who is gripped by his personal mission, deeply drawn to God and moved by the problems of the times and the afflictions of the people. In ordinary times marked by a bourgeois lifestyle, the ideal of a priest might very well have been the trustworthy administrator and functionary. However, in his view, times of upheaval and radical change demanded a "type of prophetic priest" (cf. J. Kentenich. Der apokalyptische Priester [The apocalyptic priest], retreat for priests 1940. Notes by Konrad Held, p. 15).

The prophetic priest that Father Kentenich aspired to and embodied is guided by a practical belief in God's providence. He makes himself dependent on the "law of the open door" which Father Kentenich formulated with reference to Pauline thinking (1 Cor 16:9; 2 Cor 2:12; Col 4:3).

Also in the spirit of Pauline thinking, Father Kentenich considered the priest a messenger of grace. He expressed this concept early on in a sermon he delivered in 1929 on the occasion of a newly ordained priest's first holy Mass. He himself understood his priestly life not primarily from a liturgical perspective but rather approached it in the spirit of a prophetic service of proclamation and the interpretation of the times. He was a messenger of God's grace and God's love.

The Prophetic Priest

From: J. Kentenich, Letter 1958

From the beginning, faith in Divine Providence with its instinctive sense of detecting the divine and its instinctive certainty of discerning the supernatural has simply been the atmosphere in which I have lived and worked. On this basis, I have viewed connections and made decisions. At all times, it has been the signal which indicated God's plans to me, prompted and encouraged me to undertake their implementation boldly. All this had taken on such dimensions that the most daring death leaps for my mind, will, and heart connected with them have virtually become second nature to me. They have always been and simply are to this day the normal course of action for me; in fact, they are the most natural thing in the world so that I am not even quite content without these death leaps.

Someone who had studied the type and extent of my faith in Divine Providence from a historical perspective wrote to me that he had come to the conclusion: [Because of my faith in Divine Providence], the law of the open door often forcibly broke through all ordinary barriers and crossed over into the area of a discerning vision in the actual sense of prophecy. . . .

I must admit that this observation strikes a chord and suggests connections which had not occurred to me until now.

It is true, for decades I have emphasized, both in my terminology and in my private and public activity, the prophetic type of priest in contrast to the complacent and bureaucratic type. With untiring zeal, I have made every effort to bear witness to and realize the prophetic type of priest wherever I had an opportunity. One has to keep in mind, however, that I have always only referred to a prophetic role in the wider sense of the word; that is to say, I am thinking of a type of priest who is characterized by his passionate commitment to God and to humanity, to responding to the times and to fulfilling his mission; a type of priest who has broken away from a bourgeois, self-complacent lifestyle or a formalistic, pedantic way of life and work.

How significant is here the divine intervention in every person's life through the law of the open door! How significant is the fervor and the persistent, imperturbable consistency with which this type of priest seeks to move God, his word and wish into the center while disregarding personal honor and well-being in order to pave the way for the times and people to implement God's plans for the newest shores. . . .

Against this background, I may and will and must re-emphasize: Schoenstatt and I have always wanted to be a *Providentia child per eminentiam*; nothing more and nothing less. Schoenstatt has never fancied a different role and never pretended to be anything else.

The Priest and his Belief in Divine Providence

From: J. Kentenich, Retreat for priests in the Marienau, Schoenstatt 1951

The priest who believes in Divine Providence is a priest who constantly seeks to live in union with the God of life. To be more specific, he is

1. a clear-sighted priest,
2. a daring priest,
3. a priest sure of victory.

A clear-sighted priest – a priest with clear ideas, discernment, and vision. He has sources of knowledge unknown to others. He is like a *"Spoekenkieker,"* a psychic, a person who has second sight and sees things other people do not see. *Justus meus ex fide vivit* – The one who is righteous will live by faith (Rom 1:17). Practically speaking, he will live by the truth: Nothing is a coincidence, everything is God's kind providence. The circumstances may be ever so chaotic, the priest with faith in God's providence will say: God has put me into this situation, and so it will be all right. This priest knows that he has his place in God's plan for the universe. All who come to my school might not outshine others in knowledge, but they will excel at being children of faith in God's providence.

St. Paul sees everything so very clearly. He puts his faith in the law affecting all life, the law of the open door. We want to go wherever God opens a door for us. This is practical faith in Divine Providence.

In essence it means: God speaks to me through circumstances. That is why I must learn to interpret signs. This is my life's task. God's far-reaching view spans the centuries, the millennia. As a small creature I have a small part to play. Therefore, I must stand in divine light, not merely in a general and vague sense, but in the here and now, in my circumstances.

How does our Lord make us aware of this? He says: Not a hair of your head. . . (Luke 21:18). How important was this to his audience? Jewish faith in Divine Providence had been influenced by a God of fatalism. But Jesus gave a heart to the clear-sighted God. The Jewish religion of his day was convinced that the merciful God guided the people as a nation and those who represented them, but not the individual. According to the words of Jesus, God's plan of wisdom, love, and omnipotence includes not only each individual person but also every tiny detail of this person's life.

Think of the parable of the woman who had lost a coin. What is the gist of it, the point of comparison? The economist and the entrepreneur would say, she should work and then she will make more money than she lost. But Jesus is saying: Look how the heavenly Father cares for each individual. It is similar in the parable of the lost sheep (Luke 15:3 ff.). The heavenly Father cares for each one; in fact, he acts as though the 99 did not exist at all. These truths were second nature to our grandparents and great-grandparents. We professors have lost that. We are able to talk about it, but our knowledge has not formed our lives.

We are used to seeing only the secondary cause, not the Primary Cause. For example: Someone has offended me. I do not see the Primary Cause, I do not see the Person of God, but only the secondary cause, the person who has offended me. Otherwise I would remain calmer and live a different life. Faith in Divine Providence directs everything back to the kind, wise, and almighty hand of God. I must strengthen my conviction that God holds me and my destiny in his hands. God directs everything in such a way that the plan he made for me and our family will be implemented.

In this light it is easier for us to understand our family. It was not created in accordance with a vision coming straight from heaven. Simple faith in God's providence alone was the force behind it. This gives rise to the concrete question: How does this clear-sighted view affect everyday life?

1. We want to learn how to see God everywhere, how to see him in faith; how to discover him in all things as the Primary Cause behind the secondary cause. This must be like a golden thread.

2. We want to speak lovingly with God in all circumstances.

3. Out of faith and love, we want to make sacrifices for him. This is everyday sanctity in a nutshell: *Deum quaerere, invenire, diligere in omnibus tam rebus tam hominibus.* (To seek, find, and love God in all things and in all people.) The human person who flees from God must become a person who is "addicted" to God. The person who lives a holy life is holy; the person who eats, sleeps, and speaks in a holy manner is holy, not the person who has holy dreams and a holy imagination. When we drink from the sources of the liturgy, our goal must be to revolve more steadily around the God of everyday life, not the life of a professor, not the life of a parish priest, not the life of a financial administrator. I must see and seek the God of *my* life. I must do so *in the here and now,* this is what I must learn. I must practice this piety anew.

For a priest to become clear-sighted, daring, and sure of victory, he must be grounded in faith in Divine Providence and possess a supernatural orientation.

A Messenger of Grace

*From: J. Kentenich, Address at the first holy Mass of
Fathers Bezler, Fischer, and Mutzenbach, Schoenstatt,
July 4, 1929*

May I express the thoughts I have just presented by
means of a different remembrance card of this first holy
Mass? One of us, the priest who is now celebrating holy
Mass, chose the following text: "My life has little value
unless I accomplish my priestly task and fulfill the
mission our Lord Jesus has given me – to proclaim the
good news, the message of God's grace."

A new priestly destiny is about to begin. Central to this
new priestly destiny is the momentous lifelong task to
proclaim the good news of God's grace. Grace! What is
grace? We know that grace is participation in divine life.
What is grace? Grace is participation, it is the
incorporation into the Body of Christ.

Our young priest wants to proclaim the good news of
grace. This means, he wants to have a totally supernatural
attitude. Those who are familiar with his past know how
suddenly, virtually overnight, his priestly vocation was
about to be shattered because of physical illness; they
will understand that he, like perhaps none of the other
newly ordained priests, owes to grace that he is a priest

today, that he may stand at this altar. That's why he wants to be a messenger of grace throughout his priestly life.

Grace is participation in the life of Christ. It is a priest's task to restore this divine life wherever it has been lost. It is a priest's daily task to offer to God this membership in Christ, this union with Christ, in fact to offer all who are united with Christ as one great sacrifice of praise and oblation. Shouldn't we take this opportunity today and admire the glories of the Blessed Mother under this threefold aspect as conveyed by our young priests? Receiving divine life! This life consists in the mysterious connection and union with Christ. This connection, this union is restored and maintained for the mind through faith, and for the will and the heart through love. Therefore, it is the task of all priests, and it becomes the lifelong task of our newly ordained priests in particular, to consume themselves so that this union with Christ be maintained in human souls through faith and sincere, tender love.

How great is God, how great is Christ! He instituted the priesthood so that priests might preserve the very life which he himself gave to the world; so that priests might uphold all those who are incorporated into him and preserve them in this incorporation forever. How great is Christ, how great is God that through the ministry of his priests he wants to bring back to life those who died. Where divine life atrophied and died, it is the priest who by administering the sacraments works the miracle and brings the dead back to life. That's how he populates heaven. He thus sees to it that God, that Christ keeps in constant contact with the world. Because the priest with all his thoughts and hopes, his actions and feelings is, so to speak, completely thrust into Christ, into the Mystical Christ on this earth, he also takes all the members of Christ along to heaven. Where he makes this offering, he offers not only himself, he offers not only Christ – the historical and the Eucharistic Christ – but he offers all the members of Christ's Mystical Body to the heavenly Father.

The joyful message of grace! A new priestly destiny is about to begin. The center of this destiny is the task of the Apostle Paul. It was his life's task to be a messenger of divine grace. How happy the parents and siblings of our newly ordained priest must be; above all the parents, who gave him natural life. From now on, they will receive divine life from him.

Those who have cared for his physical growth, may from now on refer to him in all their difficulties: Almighty God, we have given him to you; through him you must now give us your divine life. You must take care that he will fulfill his life's task in our family, among our children and grandchildren. Through him you must take care that divine, supernatural life will never die in our ranks. – Messenger of grace! That's how he stands before us today.

Should I repeat it and ask: To whom does he owe the revelation of God's glories? We read the second text: "Mary, Mother of Divine Grace, pray for your priests." The Blessed Mother has been his Mother in the past. She has been the Mother of Divine Grace. Everything noble and great that we see before us today may be traced back to her whom we love, to her who has played such an important role in our lives too.

Orientation to the Good Shepherd

Do you want my work: Adsum!
Do you want the slow wasting away
of all my mental powers: Adsum!
Do you want my death: Adsum!
Only see to it that
all whom you have entrusted to me
will love our Lord
and learn to live and die for him.

Joseph Kentenich
Gestapo prison in Koblenz, January 5, 1942

One of the fundamental and inspiring texts on the formation of priests in the recent past was the post-synodal Apostolic Exhortation PASTORES DABO VOBIS by Pope John Paul II in the spring of 1992. It portrays the image of the priest by basing it on the biblical motif of the shepherd, envisioning the priest as "a sacramental representation of Jesus Christ – the head and shepherd" (Pastores dabo vobis 15).

This theological view and the orientation to Jesus Christ as the Good Shepherd runs like a golden thread through the message and the retreats of Joseph Kentenich. He encouraged his confreres to make this biblical image their own and to understand it increasingly as the source of their priestly identity. At the same time, it was a fundamental concern of his that people should personally and tangibly experience the care and love which the Good Shepherd lavishes upon humanity. In his deep devotion to his followers, he was ready to give up his freedom, even to lay down his life if only all entrusted to him "will love our Lord and learn to live and die for him" (Adsum-Prayer, January 1942).

With St. Paul, Father Kentenich understood a priest's devotion in his pastoral ministry as a fatherly and motherly service. Even though during his own childhood and youth he had never experienced the loving care of his father, as a priest he became a father to countless people and an authentic transparency of the Father God. The way he carried out his priestly service gave people a sense of belonging and security; he made them feel at home in the world of God once more. He inspired and influenced many of his confreres to model their priestly life and ministry on the Good Shepherd and to embody the spirit of priestly fatherliness.

Jesus – a Shepherd's Love and a Shepherd's Care

From: J. Kentenich. Eighth talk from the USA Tertianship,
Madison, July 23, 1952

Perhaps we do well – if only to think of something different – to use the opportunity and dwell for a moment on the parable of the Good Shepherd (Jn 10:11-18).

The Good Shepherd ! Our Lord chose the image of the Good Shepherd to characterize himself, but indirectly he also characterized the Father. The Good Shepherd is the model. I should become his image, his transparency. This gives you enough connections toward above and toward below. I will sketch the image with a few central ideas and leave it to you to review and continue the train of thought.

You have to differentiate between the general characterization and the individual virtues of a shepherd.

Our Lord indicated the general characterization with the striking words: "I am the good shepherd" (Jn 10:11-14). When we reflect on the circumstances in which our Lord said this, we are justified in shifting the accent. Then the statement can be: First, "I am the *good* shepherd." Second: "I am *the* good shepherd."

What does the shift in accent indicate? You have to remember whom our Lord addressed when he used the image, when he taught the lesson. The Jews, the

Israelites. They were well acquainted with the Old Testament; they knew that already in the Old Testament the image of the shepherd, of the good shepherd, was used countless times. You remember the whole history of Israel: First, God ruled over Israel through the patriarchs, the prophets, and the priests. Then the people became restless; they compared themselves with neighboring nations and observed that they had kings. And so the people demanded: We, too, want to have a king. God granted their request.

As the prophets of old tell us, soon the people began complaining about the manner in which both the king as well as the priests guided the people; the image of the bad shepherd was the subject of their account, time and time again. What did these shepherds want? They demanded wool, they demanded the milk of the sheep; they cared desperately little about the sheep themselves. Then God prophesied: I will send you the shepherd. We understand. What shepherd did he refer to? I don't want to dwell on the thought, you can think about it yourselves.

When our Lord said: I am the good shepherd ordained from all eternity, he referred to the shepherd announced in the Old Testament. This is I. "I am the good shepherd."

Look, my dear Confreres, you can observe how clearly our Lord portrayed himself as a personality; as a personality ordained and foreordained from eternity; indeed, as a personality.

And so, I think, we also have to make sure that we do not depersonalize our Lord and that we do not depersonalize the Father God. Second, can't we all say in a certain sense: I, too, am *the* shepherd? I am the provincial, I am the rector, I don't know what office it is. Look, in the light of faith – I do not even need so very much light of faith – I may tell myself: The fate of my community has been placed into my hands for so and so many years. I am *the* shepherd of my community, foreseen from eternity for this period of time.

Do you notice what this is all about? It is a thought which we in this age of herd mentality cannot stress seriously enough and often enough: an awareness of my personal mission in spite of my weakness. I have a unique, personal mission, and no one else has exactly the same. You see, there is this constant struggle to overcome the feeling of being no more than a number. Most of the time, we are just numbers, we feel like a number. Remember what I told you about Duns Scotus. At least take the thought with you and try to internalize it: *Deus quaerit condiligentes se* (God searches for persons who love what he loves). The issue is always the same, only seen and considered from a different angle: We have to learn how to overcome our tendency toward a herd mentality; we must learn to become much more ourselves and unfold our self-identities.

You see, [we must become] *the* person God intended us to be from eternity for these times, a person who matters. Hence it depends on me what will become of the province. It depends on me what is going to develop in Madison. It depends on me what is going to develop in Washington – wherever my task will take me. We may not fall asleep and say: "What do I care! Let others worry about it." When "Reservists are on leave, they are on leave indeed." That's a petty excuse. Remember what we said about the passivists who let history run its course; the activists who shake up history, and those who make and create history. Look, a person who believes in Divine Providence knows that Almighty God needs instruments. He needs *me.* He does not want to rule the world by himself. True, we know about God's absolute efficacy. We know that God can do all things by himself, but we also know that God does not want to do all things by himself.

And so, you must understand: I am *the* good shepherd. Here we see *the* good shepherd, *the* person destined from eternity – our Lord as the image of the heavenly Father.

Then: "I am the *good* shepherd." – This is the same thought often described in the Old Testament. What is the good shepherd like? He does not care for the sheep just because of their wool, he does not care for the sheep just because of their milk; in other words, he does not forget about the sheep themselves, he does not ignore the well-being of the sheep in order to profit from them. No, the good shepherd even lays down his life for his sheep;

he unselfishly always seeks to serve the well-being of others. Our Lord says: "I am the good shepherd," and he is a reflection of the Father. "Philip, whoever has seen me has seen the Father" (Jn 14:9). Can you see that the description we are talking about always refers to the same idea: The God of love has the reins in his hand? The God of love sacrifices himself for our sake.

With that we have a general characterization. If I want to be an image of God, then I must try in my own way to be a good shepherd and I may not do my job primarily because of financial gain. Of course, I may also work for monetary gain, but it must never be the primary reason. The main reason must always be to emulate the good shepherd as he characterized himself.

If you look at the individual virtues – I will do so just briefly and quickly – you will notice how our Lord characterized himself and thereby pointed to two virtues in particular – a shepherd's love and a shepherd's care.

A shepherd's love. What makes me think of the shepherd's love? Our Lord characterized himself when he said: "I know my own (and my own know me), as the Father knows me and I know the Father" (Jn 10:14 f.). You have to realize what a tremendous ideal this is. How does the Father know the Son and the Son know the Father? This is not just an intellectual knowing; it is a loving embrace. Look, this is how I should know my own. Consequently, our Lord knows me the way the Father knows him, and he knows the Father; he knows about every little thing. This is the pivotal point. He knows about every little thing. And every little thing is present in his thoughts and recorded in his plans. You see, here we see a shepherd's love.

The shepherd's love is so immense that it can be likened to the love between the Father and the Son within the Blessed Trinity. However, this should also be the standard for me. If I want to reflect Eternal Love, then my fundamental attitude should essentially be to acquire, to grow in a shepherd's love, not to acquire a superabundance of intellectual knowledge. True, this may also be, but it is not the main point.

What should this love of a shepherd be like? It should really be a very personal love. In this connection we might recall how Alban Stolz in his day defined education. The definition applies extraordinarily well to us. What is education according to his definition? To maintain a living contact. What does maintaining a living contact mean? It is one single stream of life. The stream of life does not only flow through me but also through my followers. Maintaining a living contact – let me be very down-to-earth and make it specific. I take a lively and sincere interest in every small thing concerning my followers; put playfully – whether someone has a corn on his toe or in his soul. Do you understand the ideal meant here? If the love between the Father and the Son within the Blessed Trinity is the ideal and if our Lord has this same tender, caring love for us and if we are supposed to be his images, please understand the implications.

Combining Fatherly and Motherly Service like St. Paul

From: J. Kentenich, Krise um Regierungsformen, Milwaukee, Wisconsin, USA. September 1961 [Crisis of Forms of Government]

The description of the Pauline ideal of authority is a certain highpoint. From the beginning we have kept this ideal in sight and to this day we have persistently reached out for it.

[The Pauline ideal] is a unique combination of fatherliness and motherliness which expresses a willingness to serve selflessly in the most perfect possible way. We have to keep in mind the diverse types of rootlessness now and in the future, and we have to anticipate that the interior life, the psychological health of future generations might be in a state of great inner neglect. To bring about this harmony [the combination of fatherly and motherly service] in a person will present the modern educator with a tremendous challenge.

The topic of the retreat refers to Paul's self-portrayal in First Thessalonians and his Letter to the Galatians. These words give us a sense of Paul's helplessness as he struggles to find the right words in order to express his fundamental attitude as an educator and pastor of souls. At times, he describes his educational task as a motherly service, at times as a fatherly service. If we want to do justice to both tasks, we have little choice but to say that Paul displays the most perfect possible combination of fatherliness and motherliness.

Holzner (Joseph Holzner, Paulus, Freiburg 1937) characterizes the self-portrayal of the Apostle to the Gentiles in the Letter to the Thessolonians as follows.

"(He) was not only a missionary, a conqueror, but also a pastor. He knew how to strengthen and safeguard what he had conquered for the Lord. He was not set on quick, dazzling success. As a missionary he compared himself to a 'circumspect master builder'; in his pastoral ministry, to a 'father' who keeps his children on the straight and narrow in a strict yet kind way; to a 'mother' who loves her child of sorrow most; to a 'wet nurse' who cares for the infant in her care."

The text of the Apostle's Letter is so clear that after this portrayal no other commentary is necessary.

Paul writes: ". . . though we might have made demands as apostles of Christ. But we were gentle among you, like a nurse taking care of her children. So, being affectionately desirous of you, we were ready to share with you not only the Gospel of God but also our own selves, because you had become very dear to us. For you remember our labor and toil, brethren; we worked night and day, that we might not burden any of you, while we preached to you the Gospel of God. You are witnesses, and God also, how holy and righteous and blameless was our behavior to you believers; for you know how, like a father with his children, we exhorted each one of you and encouraged you and charged you to walk in a manner worthy of God, who calls you into his own kingdom and glory" (1 Thess 2:7-12).

In his Letter to the Galatians, Paul describes his motherly function of guiding, of counseling souls and educating with these words, which are truly classic: "My little children, with whom I am again in travail until Christ be formed in you. I could wish to be present with you now and to change my tone, for I am perplexed about you" (Gal 4:19).

Holzner comments on this text: "After having defeated his adversaries with the sharpest weapon, his line of reasoning, Paul suddenly becomes gentle like a mother and gives free rein to his feelings: Like a mother for her children, I would gladly suffer labor pains for you again and speak like a mother speaks to her children! It is strange, indeed, how this man unites such polarity within himself: logic hard like steel, unyielding will power, and the tender feelings of a mother. It is the picture of the mother hen used by Christ. Paul's friends must have been caught up in the moving influence of this Christ-like love. . ."

Creating a Spiritual Home for those Entrusted to him

From: J. Kentenich, Kampf um die wahre Freiheit,
Retreat for priests, Schoenstatt, January 7-10, 1946
[The struggle for true freedom]

We ourselves should be a home for our followers. Unless we succeed in making the people feel at home in us, feel that they may turn to their pastor with all their problems and that he has empathy, we will often fail. Adolf Kolping, who certainly knew his people very well, was fully aware of people's attachment to their priests. He wrote: "That's the reason why our people are so very attached to a priest even when they change over to Socialism and Communism: Teary-eyed they secretly glance at the Catholic priest." A priest must be a father for his parish community, not a grandfather. I must make the problems of the people my own. Alban Stolz said: "To educate means to maintain a living contact." I must assimilate the entire stream of life of my parish community. A stream of life also flows forth from me. The contact has to be more than ideological. "I am the good shepherd. I know my own and my own know me, as the Father knows me and I know the Father."

We have to accept the love from our followers, from those in our care. We have to get used to that. When we are young, it makes us feel uncomfortable. As we get older, we are afraid this love could be too human. When it comes to education through love, it is true: Absolutely nothing, not even in education, is entirely safe and without danger. But it is just as dangerous when I appear like a block of wood and only point to heaven. St. Paul demonstrates what authentic Catholic educational wisdom is all about. He calls himself *forma gregis* (the model for his flock). We are marked by the age of individualism, but we exclude ourselves from it. We do so in words, but we do not act accordingly. We stand between God and humanity. Human beings bond with human beings. Human beings come to God through other human beings. This is the healthiest education. Hence I have to accept the love of my followers with sincerity and simplicity. On the other hand, I may not pursue someone in order to win their love. If I am the model, if I am the form my followers are to be configured to, if Christ is the form for me, then the normal way is for a human being to bond with other human beings and to take them along into the heart of God. We have to admit ever so often that countless people love God so little because they love people so little. A healthy love for God depends on healthy human love.

In this direction, St. Augustine solved a great many perplexities. It sounds strange to us today when he said: The central organ for faith is love. For example, if I have received noble love from someone, really deep love that is, won't it be easy for me to understand what Holy Scripture says about God? If I did not have this experience, what does the idea, the concept of God mean to me? It is only something abstract. The image of God is shaped by the human image. Why is it that people often do not connect with God as a Father? Because they did not experience an earthly father. Love is the central organ for faith. We want to simply and naturally accept people's love if they offer it to us. In his testament Don Bosco wrote to his sons: "If you want the children in your care to strive for individual virtues, you have to see to it that they love you!" This is educational wisdom in a nutshell. He said: "You have to love them, but you must also show your love to them." Love is awakened by love. I must love in a healthy way.

Of course, once love has been awakened, I may not be a thief or an adulterer. I have to carefully pass on the love and reverence given me. A sound organism of attachments, an interior sense of belonging demands physical self-containment and integrity so that love can be transmitted into the heart of God. The *regula tactus* (the rule of contact) must be observed. For us priests it means: to be interiorly ingenuous and exteriorly completely intact. This applies not only regarding girls, but also boys.

A noble human being who has found a home in God must also become a home to many people. We are a home for one another. Being a home for another person includes a task. Giving a home to another person demands selflessness of me. St. Paul speaks of the "constant pressure from people." He wishes to be "all things to all people." If we are able to give ourselves selflessly to others and give others a home, it will also be easy to make them feel at home in God. If something is missing, one link in the chain is broken. See to it that people become a home for each other.

This applies to the family as well. Every family must assimilate and internalize the words of our "Home Song": ". . . where they glow and shelter one another and flow as one into the heart of God; where streams of love well forth with might to quench the thirst of the world for love." This must become a reality in every family. Of course, in practice every family must also bear with each other. The more we mean to each other, the more difficult it may be to put up with some things. "The family table is a table of enjoyment but also of sacrifice." We must give each other a sense of belonging and security .

If the members of a religious family wish each other well, an atmosphere of warmth will be created. Being together constantly, smoking, eating and drinking together, etc., does not make a family. The family table should ultimately be a table of sacrifice, a table of love. Decisive is the deep manly realization: We who are gathered here serve one and the same task. This is especially important for a community of men. That's why we as the Federation of men have one great task: to meet each other with benevolence, to stand together and to stick together. If we only see ideas but do not work together for great goals, the community will fall apart. How do we make our people interiorly free? By giving them a home. How do we ourselves become interiorly free? By consuming ourselves in the fulfillment of our task.

Challenged to Live Apostolic Holiness

Bind me, Lord,
and have mercy on me.
Bind me to . . .

Detach me, Lord,
and have mercy on me.
Detach me from . . .

Unite me, Lord,
and have mercy on me.
Unite me with . . .

Cincture Prayer
Joseph Kentenich

Both in the large retreats for priests as well as in the formation of the communities of priests belonging to his movement, Joseph Kentenich placed great importance on a spirituality appropriate for secular priests. Even though he respected the specific spirituality of the orders, he suggested an apostolic ideal of holiness which is oriented to the work of priests among the people, to the work of priests in the world. His words and characterizations were unambiguous as he pointed at flaws in carrying out the priestly office. He was specific in mentioning hazardous and erroneous methods by name without being reproachful.

Joseph Kentenich was passionate about showing his confreres the ideal time and time again. He tried to kindle their desire to strive for priestly holiness. For this purpose, he would invite his audience to go into the school of St. Paul, who to him embodied the ideal of apostolic holiness.

His primary concern was the spiritual life of priests which would enable them to carry out their pastoral duties. It would also develop their personal charisma and increase their apostolic fruitfulness.

The Ideal of Apostolic Holiness

*From: J. Kentenich. Die moderne priesterliche
Werktagsheiligkeit. Retreat for priests, Schoenstatt 1939
[Everyday sanctity for the modern priest]*

We must personify the distinctly apostolic saint, and this
is really the unique grace of a priest. St. Thomas says: "I
do not become a priest in order to become holy
personally; this is only a secondary task. Primarily, I
become a priest in order to sanctify the world." Every
priest must be a markedly apostolic person.

What is my task as a Schoenstatt priest? Schoenstatt
emphasizes in a special way all that is asked of a priest
by his ordination. Schoenstatt really does not add much
that is new.

We must develop a distinct and justified pride in our
priestly state. Then all the good a priest ever
accomplished will make us very happy. Let us gladly
read the biographies of great priests; yet we also need to
have the courage to face the other side of the coin. The
ideal is an extraordinarily high degree of apostolic
holiness.

What is the distortion of a priest? We speak of a *"Pfaffe"*
(German derogatory term for a priest), of a moralizing
priest, a pharisaic priest, and a hysterical priest. . .

A priest becomes a distortion, a caricature, when he is puffed up with conceit, when his own self stands in the center and humility ends. A priest must be an *alter Christus* (another Christ). I may not primarily think of my own well-being – my physical, financial, spiritual-intellectual well-being. I am united with Christ, I belong to Christ. There are priests who work as though they had taken a vow of servitude. Their life is characterized by the apostolate. The caricature burns incense to his own person, he mistakes himself for God, he refers to God but means himself.

The moralizing priest: This is a petty-minded, fussy, nagging type. He settles for a minimum of effort. Where is his great drive for the world apostolate?

The pharisaic type: Important to him is the exterior appearance of everyday sanctity and justice. He is not interested in a person's attitude. He is hardened, he leaves much blood on the carpet.

The hysterical priest: This is the "changeling," a fickle person. He lacks vigor. He has no ambitions and aspirations. These priests take pride in being vital and enterprising, when in reality they merely have a vitalistic attitude. Today this, tomorrow that. They lack one great, final goal on which they focus, to which they are oriented. We Schoenstatt members are not primarily "a club for self-sanctification," we are an apostolic movement. Some time in the future, we will have to emphasize this much more in every respect.

102

Becoming a Golden Priest

From: J. Kentenich. Retreat for Schoenstatt Fathers, Schoenstatt, November 4-8, 1966

There is not only a first conversion in the Church but also a second. Applied to ourselves, we like to compare ourselves with the Church: There is a first and a second Schoenstatt conversion. What is the first and what is the second Schoenstatt conversion? You realize, we should really take for granted that by the time the tertianship ends, we may, can and must acknowledge and gratefully confirm: We have experienced the second Schoenstatt conversion. Our goal must be set high.

What, then, is the nature of the first and the second conversion? I will use a triad of expressions to help me. We talked about some of these expressions on various occasions in the past. One expression is from an American cardinal (James Gibbons). According to him, there are the iron person, the silver person, and the golden person; iron priests, silver priests and golden priests; (consequently) there are iron Schoenstatt priests, silver Schoenstatt priests, golden Schoenstatt priests. What is the difference? Let me first explain the individual expressions.

The iron priest is content with doing what he has to do. Case closed.

The silver priest strives for heroism. But his heroism across-the-board is mainly based on mere natural motivation. Let's say on ambition; he wants to accomplish something. We know that such motives will always play a role in the advancement of humanity and the development of the human person. But if that is all, I might be a sacrificial person, a sacrificial priest. True, he is a valuable priest in the eyes of God, but not the most valuable.

The golden priest. We keep using the same expressions instead of coining new ones. This is the priest who has been drawn into the supernatural world with his whole being. Of this priest it can be said: "My righteous one shall live by faith" (Heb 10:38). He is supernatural through and through. He is completely at home in the other world and therefore applies the standards of the other world; he applies them to the cross and suffering, to disappointments in people, to himself, to those in authority, to the whole world. You understand what all this means.

When St. Paul likes to speak about boasting, ask yourself what he boasts of? He boasts of having been caught up to heaven. He boasts. What does he boast of? He glories in the cross of Christ that he may carry (cf. Gal 6:14). He boasts of his weakness (cf. 2 Cor 11:30; 12:9 f.). This is the otherworldly person, the supernatural, the golden person.

Now apply it to Schoenstatt. I think you understand what is meant.

What is the iron Schoenstatt priest like? I could also ask: What is a Schoenstatt priest like after his first conversion? In summary, we may probably say that the iron Schoenstatt priest is the priest who experienced his first Schoenstatt conversion. He is what we called before the iron and the silver Schoenstatt priest. The iron [Schoenstatt] priest just fulfills his most necessary duties. The silver priest might well be heroic, may make great and greatest sacrifices, but the final motive is a purely natural motive, ambition or whatever. When it comes to the second conversion, we meet the golden priest whose only motto is: My citizenship is in heaven in every respect. Set your minds on things that are above (cf. Phil 3:20; Col 3:1-2). Things that are on earth have little meaning and little value. Standards that are common practice at the throne of the eternal God are also common practice in the colony of heaven [here below].

We ask again: Are we as family on the way to being a colony of heaven? Are we on the way to becoming really and truly golden Schoenstatt priests across-the-board? When we glance once more at our relationship to the family as a whole, don't we have to say: When it comes down to it, couldn't and shouldn't we really be an elite of golden Schoenstatt priests? Whatever we lack in being golden priests is an extraordinary deficiency that affects our whole activity. According to the law of paradigm, shouldn't we as *pars motrix* (moving part), that is, as the life-giving, guiding and leading force of the family, [be golden Schoenstatt priests]! This is also implied in the law we have mentioned before. We remember how important it is for us to be a magnificent embodiment of the ideal. Keeping all this in mind, we should indeed embody the ideal – the ideal of being a gathering and assembly, a family of golden Schoenstatt priests. To the extent that we – according to the law of paradigm – represent, strive to represent this type of priest, the whole family will be safe. To the extent that we make mistakes and fail in this regard. . . . Please hear what all this means: We are co-founders in the actual sense of the word. As co-founders we also share in being the soul. Being co-founders and sharing in being the soul also means to exemplify what God expects more or less of the whole family.

And so, I may repeat that it is really important to go into the school of our family history. You may be reminded and believe that the family history of the last years, of this past decade, has truly helped us to become a community, to embody a type of priest, of whom it can be said: They have experienced a second conversion, they have truly become golden Schoenstatt priests, golden Schoenstatt members. Think about it. How many offered their lives during these past years and how often God accepted their life's offering! For what purpose? For the existence and fruitfulness of our small family.

Living as Vessels of the Spirit

From: J. Kentenich. Seelenfuehrerkurs Mystik, Schoenstatt,
August 30 - September 3, 1927 [Course in pastoral ministry]

Dear Confreres of the Federation. In jest we sometimes call each other "spiritual vessel." Ask yourself what the expression really means. What does it tell us? Don't expect me to develop the ideas in detail. I just mention them to loosen the subsoil in your soul for tomorrow.

In the Litany of Loreto, we have an anthology of the most wonderful titles honoring Mary. This litany is quite old. Some trace the name to the town of Loreto where it originated – or rather – where, according to tradition, it was prayed. You might be aware of the fact that this litany became an established prayer in Germany through Peter Canisius.

Most of the titles are easy to understand, especially the first part. The glories, the titles of honor of the Blessed Mother, are highlighted: Mother of God, Virgin, etc. They point at the power and kindness of the Blessed Mother. . . The second part contains some invocations which are more difficult to understand. In order to grasp their meaning we need to be somewhat acquainted and familiar with Holy Scripture because they are taken from Old Testament accounts. This is true of the invocation:

Vas spirituale

What does the title mean? I have to consult the Scriptures to see how the title was used. *Vas* is the symbolic description of the human person, now the body, now the whole person? We are reminded of the words of St. Paul (cf. 2 Cor 4:7). At issue is the gift which we carry in a fragile vessel. Here the body is called a fragile vessel. But the expression is also applied to the whole person. God said to Ananias, referring to Paul: "He is a chosen instrument of mine" (Acts 9:15). (The Latin translation of the Vulgate is: *"Vas electionis."*) The whole person has been sanctified by God in a special way and accepted as his very own possession.

When we invoke Mary as *vas spirituale,* we recall that she, too, was a chosen instrument, even much more so than Paul and the other great Apostles. *Vas spirituale!* A spiritual vessel. . . . Who chose Mary as a vessel, as an instrument? The Holy Spirit! *Vas spirituale:* She appears before us as *causa efficiens* (the efficient cause) in the hands of the Holy Spirit. . . .

For what purpose was she chosen as a spiritual vessel? For what purpose? A completely spiritual purpose. The miracle of the incarnation was to take place in her. She should cooperate in the redemption and sanctification of the world. She was the human link used by the Holy Spirit in order to make redemption possible, to make it a reality and bring it to completion.

1. Mary was an exquisite vessel.

Let us take a close look at Mary. She was filled with the Spirit of God many times over. How the Holy Spirit descended upon her, upon her soul, and freed her from original sin! How he glorified her body, and preserved it from the sting of concupiscence! . . . And what did he use Mary for? Imagine the great task of the Blessed Mother!

2. A generous and willing vessel and instrument.

As *causa prima* (primary cause) God works with the help of the *causa secunda* (secondary cause). He uses it for his plans. However, in using efficient causes he adjusts himself to the nature of the particular efficient cause. After creating the human person with a free will, he respects this free will. For this reason God asks and pleads for a person's consent. The Blessed Mother, too, was asked for her consent. And the *vas spirituale* said yes: Fiat. Let it be done!

3. A very effective vessel and instrument.

Think of the effectiveness of her fiat (let it be done to me!) at the annunciation (this "fiat" had an impact on the entire redemption), the effectiveness of her fiat beneath the cross as well as the law of the universal mediation of grace. All are dependent on this instrument that mediates all graces. . . .

Vas spirituale – ora pro nobis!

This title has ever so rich a meaning. Of course, we are happy about this special characteristic. Of course, we turn to her in our personal problems. We are in need of her gifts; without them we would perish. We have to come to a deeper and clearer understanding of this thought. The Blessed Mother was a *vas spirituale*. I, too, am a *vas spirituale*. But is that really so? If so, what then? Then it must be true that God's Holy Spirit has also chosen me for his spiritual purposes and tasks. Is that so?

Didn't the Holy Spirit sign me with a special character in baptism? What is the purpose of baptism? I become a member of Christ, a child of God. The Holy Spirit takes my soul and makes it his property. Also remember that he infuses love of God.

Above all, think of ordination. Doesn't it give me a participation in the high priestly character of the God-Man? The task of the great God-Man has become my task; a spiritual-intellectual task. And so, I am ontologically a *vas spirituale*.

Now please recall the primary, fundamental principle of our moral acts; in fact, of our whole striving for holiness: *ordo essendi est ordo agendi*. The objective order of being must be the norm for my subjective moral order, for my actions, for my priestly activity and effectiveness.

St. Paul expresses the demands arising from the *ordo essendi* (order of being) for my personal living in his classic way. He piles up expressions in order to show how we, as vessels of the Spirit, should also live according to the Spirit (cf. Rom 8:4 f.). We should "put to death the deeds of the body" (cf. Rom 8:13). We should "set our minds on things that are above, not on things that are on earth" (cf. Col 3:1 f.; Phil 4:8; Eph 4:17-24). If I am a spiritual vessel in the real order of being, I also have to live a spiritual life in accordance with this order. "Walk by the Spirit . . ." (cf. Gal 5:16).

"You who belong to Christ Jesus have crucified the flesh with its passions and desires" (cf. Gal 5:24). The deepest and most important thing that we must strive for is to communicate the Holy Spirit to others in whatever we do. As *vas spirituale,* we are called to be bearers of the Spirit, and as bearers of the Spirit we should be able to awaken the Spirit everywhere.

Let us make an effort so that during these days we will gain a deeper understanding of what it means to be a *vas spirituale.* To accomplish this we must first understand the concept of *vas spirituale.* But then we must also translate this concept into life. This is a great grace, and we have to pray for it. From experience we know that we cannot do this on our own, by our own strength. Our Mother has to obtain it for us. That's why we must pray with one another for one another.

The Priest and the Blessed Mother

Our Lord has chosen you to be his priest.
In you he wants to go through the world
and bless it,
in you he wants to sacrifice,
pray, love, and suffer,
in you he wants to pasture his sheep
here on earth.
He has placed his Mother at your side,
his Mother who accompanied him
throughout his life.
Remain faithful to her
in all of life's circumstances.
She will help you bear
your burden joyfully,
she will lead you
and your spiritual children,
the souls in your pastoral care,
to the shores of eternal happiness.

Congratulations from Father Kentenich to Karl Leisner
on his priestly ordination in Dachau concentration camp
December 17, 1944

In a 1931 retreat about "The mission of priests and the mission of the laity," Father Kentenich spoke extensively about the connection between the Christian mission and the mission of the Blessed Mother. Wherever priests and the laity are actively engaged in the renewal of the world in Christ, they may and should rely on Mary's help and orient themselves by her example. Whoever wants to actively promote devotion to Mary, will enlist her with her special calling and her God-given mission. Our approach to work on behalf of the Kingdom of God and to configure the world to Christ is profoundly Marian.

Time and time again, he encouraged priests to orient themselves to Mary and to view themselves as "Marian priests" who are close to the Blessed Mother and live their lives in union with her. Father Kentenich was very happy when a young priest entrusted his priestly life entirely to Mary and began his priestly ministry in her name, as he stated in his sermon on Easter 1934 on the occasion of a newly ordained priest's first holy Mass. In this sermon he also expressed his own thoughts about a priest's inner closeness to Mary.

In 1935, on the occasion of the silver jubilee of his priestly ordination, he revealed the degree to which he himself saw and lived his priesthood in union with Mary. This particular sermon is a powerful and distinct testimony to the fruitfulness of devotion to the Blessed Mother and of committing one's priesthood to her. In a talk in 1960 in Milwaukee, on the occasion of his golden jubilee of priestly ordination, the founder expressed similar thoughts.

114

Our Method is Marian

From: J. Kentenich, Priesterliche Sendung und Laiensendung, Retreat for priests, Schoenstatt, October 11-18, 1931
[The mission of priests and the mission of the laity]

Our mission is of divine origin; the goal of this mission is divine as well. Our approach, our method? Could we also say that our method or our approach to fulfill this mission is divine?

Let us first build a bridge. Following up the closing thought of the first part, we told ourselves: Our mission is not simply a divine mission, but a divine and Marian mission. We have also realized that our goal is oriented to God and to Mary – the Marian configuration of the world to Christ. Depending on our interpretation of the word Marian, we can all agree that our approach must also be divine and Marian. A Marian approach can have a threefold meaning:

By her intercession, the Blessed Mother should help us to imprint Christ's features on the world. Catholic thinking can hardly object to this type of interpretation. Mary is the interceding omnipotence and she, above all, will understand us best.

There is a second interpretation: Marian devotion is my primary means to bring about the configuration of the world to Christ. I want to be an apostle of Marian

115

devotion and thus compel the Blessed Mother, if you will, to imprint Christ's features upon the world. *Per Mariam cum Maria et pro Maria* (through Mary, with Mary, and for Mary. [Doing it for Mary] does not mean that she is the final goal of our actions; she is the beginning. The goal is and remains the configuration of the world to Christ for the glory of the Father. There are no objections from a theological angle to carry out our pastoral service in this spirit.

In order to familiarize ourselves with the activity of the Blessed Mother, we can take a theological and a historical approach.

A theological perspective: The Blessed Mother's position within the entire plan of salvation is that of the official Christ-Bearer. Hence where Christ appears, the Blessed Mother will be nearby in some form. Where she appears, Christ is necessarily present as well. By virtue of her office, it is her task to bear Christ and to give him to the world. The Wise Men found our Lord in the arms of his Mother. So did the shepherds. This is not a coincidence; it is symbolic. The Blessed Mother appears before us: the Ave in her ears, the Magnificat on her lips, the Child in her arms, the sevenfold sword in her heart, and the tongues of fire above her head. Could we paint a more beautiful picture? Instead of Christ-Bearer, we could also call her the Birth-Giver. It is her task to give birth to Christ wherever she is allowed to do so.

People with a liturgical orientation take it for granted that the Blessed Mother is the Mediatrix of All Graces. She holds a unique position in the Church of God. Christ is the head of the Corpus Christi Mysticum (the Mystical Body of Christ), the Holy Spirit the soul, the Blessed Mother the heart. Pope Pius X called the road through Mary the simplest, surest, and most direct way toward configuring our own lives and those of others to Christ. We will have to make use of every means available if we want to make progress. It is easiest if we place the Blessed Mother in the foreground. If we want to configure the world to Christ in Mary's spirit, we also must promote self-denial and prayer. But these things are then seen in a different light. We sacrifice and pray with Mary's spirit and this Marian spirit gives our prayer to our Lord a special character. This is the essence of the Marian configuration to Christ.

A historical perspective: We have a unique collection of facts before us. Wherever the Blessed Mother appears, she does so to protect the Person of Christ. The christological battles have always been linked to the Blessed Mother. Venerating and honoring the Blessed Mother is the best rampart to protect the Person of our Lord. Where the Blessed Mother is rejected, [belief] in her Son will erode too. The words *soli Deo* (God alone) assume quite a different meaning. Some people are of the opinion that whatever is not divine should be removed from our lives. Therefore, do away with the saints, do away with the Blessed Mother! Consequently, do away with the human nature of the God-Man also! In the end, *soli* becomes sol, the sun god, nature worship. For this reason, it is important to cultivate a great devotion to Mary. Today's Eucharistic movement was preceded by a Marian movement. A person who has a deep love for Mary will always also grow in a deep love for our Lord, for the Father, and the Holy Spirit.

The third interpretation: We can all agree that if our approach is Marian, then Mary is our model. The third part of the retreat will deal with the method, the approach used to fulfill our mission. A number of paintings in the chapel might inspire us. The picture of the Good Shepherd. . . . But I could also say: I want to copy the method used to fulfill my mission from the person of the Blessed Mother. Two reasons speak in its favor. First, our modern priests are confronted with enormous difficulties in finding the right way to relate to women. Yet, woman plays an important role in a priest's life. If we use Mary's image to illustrate our pastoral ministry, we do so in order to clarify the image of woman through the image of the Blessed Mother. By seeing the image of woman ennobled in this way, we have the best rampart. The Blessed Mother shows us the ideal.

The Marian Priest

From: J. Kentenich, Der marianische Priester, Retreat for priests, Schoenstatt 1941 [The Marian Priest]

A Marian priest portrays the features of Mary in a distinct form. Similarly, we speak of an enterprising and a dedicated priest when the attributes of daring courage and passionate zeal distinguish his character.

We are used to differentiating between three degrees of Marian devotion: the ordinary, the great, and the extraordinarily great devotion to Mary. The Marian priest has an extraordinarily deep and ardent devotion to Mary.

After defining the term, let us now add two essential definitions. Our traditional definition of a Marian person or priest: In the light of faith, this person has a clear understanding of the Blessed Mother's position in the plan of salvation and acts accordingly in practical life.

In adapting the first part of this definition in the spirit of our retreat, ". . . a clear understanding of the Blessed Mother's position," we have arrived at a second essential definition: A Marian priest is a priest who has the clearest and deepest possible understanding of God's eternal original idea of the Blessed Mother and her position in the plan of salvation as well as its timely and appropriate realization; he makes this understanding practical in his love and life, even to the point of perfection.

If this is the definition of a Marian priest, wouldn't every priest have to be a Marian priest? Doubtlessly! Hence doesn't this definition express something taken for granted and thereby judged unnecessary? However, is every priest today Marian in this sense? If not, then the definition is justified.

Why should the Marian character be a matter of course for every priest? Canon 1276 CIC reads: *Bonum atque utile est Dei Servos, una cum Christo regnantes, suppliciter invocare eorumque reliquias atque imagines venerari, sed prae ceteris filiali devotione Beatissimam Virginem Mariam fideles universi prosequantur* (It is good and useful to call humbly on the servants of God who reign with Christ and to venerate their relics and images; however, above all the faithful should cultivate a childlike love for the Blessed Virgin Mary). The last words contain a certain warmth which breaks through the matter-of-fact, precise wording of the canon.

The words *prae ceteris autem* (however, above all) make it clear that devotion to Mary supercedes the veneration of all the other saints, as theology expresses with the words *dulia* and *hyperdulia*. She is the Mother of God, not merely a servant like the other saints. She is the helper and associate of Christ. Hence *filialis devotio* (childlike devotion) to Mary is appropriate. And so, a great devotion to Mary is simply required of every Catholic.

What does this involve? To begin with, we should refrain from doing whatever could grieve her, and this is especially sin. Furthermore, we should celebrate her feasts and emulate her virtues.

If this is demanded of every Catholic, how much more does it apply to priests. In his encyclical "On the Catholic Priesthood" (Dec 20, 1935), Pius XI states: "This piety should primarily be directed towards God our Father in Heaven; yet it should be extended also to the Mother of God. The priest even more than the faithful should have devotion to Our Lady, for the relation of the priest to Christ is more deeply and truly like that which Mary bears to her Divine Son" (39). Hence every priest must be markedly Marian. We speak of a Marian priest in order to make this a greater reality.

Don't we as Schoenstatt members have an outspoken devotion to Mary? Certainly, it should be so. However, this is not even enough. Since we gave a blank-check to the MTA, we at least reach for the ideal of an extraordinary devotion to Mary. The blank-check, correctly understood, includes Marian devotion according to St. Louis De Montfort, which involves an extraordinarily high degree of devotion to Mary. We have to add that giving a blank-check asks an extraordinarily high degree of ethical values. Therefore, we will have to mobilize all the driving forces inherent in Marian devotion. This presupposes that we reach out for this unique devotion to Mary.

The Beginning of a Marian Priestly Life

From: J. Kentenich, Sermon on the occasion of a newly ordained priest's first holy Mass, Schoenstatt, Easter 1934

Today the Church does not tire of singing a joyful, jubilant alleluia. We see it as a repetition of the alleluia the Blessed Mother sang on the historic resurrection day. Suffering is now over, and our Lord has now reached a certain highpoint, a certain finale in the fulfillment of his life's task. We wonder whether the Blessed Mother up above in heaven sings a new ardent, joyful alleluia. After all, she is not only the Mother of our Lord, she is also the Mother of the members of our Lord; above all, she is the Mother of priests. Hasn't the life of one of her priests, guided and protected by her motherly love, found a degree of fulfillment today? Alleluia! His efforts and worries have led him to his goal; he has reached his goal successfully.

We rejoice with the Blessed Mother. We rejoice all the more because this day marks the beginning of a Marian priestly life, the priestly life of a Schoenstatt priest.

A Marian priestly life. All who are familiar with these times, all who know that in many circles it is no longer an honor to be a Christian, a Catholic, all who know that it is even less of an honor to be a priest, will rejoice today. In spite of these difficult conditions and circumstances, a new priestly life begins here at this place [of grace]. It is a Marian priestly life.

The Blessed Mother must be seen as the source, the protection, the leader, and the goal that distinguishes this young priest's life.

United by the bonds of a tender love for Mary and a deep, noble attachment to this Marian place, we rejoice as this Marian priestly life is about to begin.

The Blessed Mother is the source of this life. May I remind you that her fiat spoken some two thousand years ago marks the first beginning and the source of the high priesthood of the God-Man? Since we believe that our priesthood in the Church is merely a continuation of this eternal high priesthood, an incorporation into this high priesthood, we will understand the meaning of the statement: Every priesthood in God's Church may and must trace its origin, its source back to the Blessed Mother. In this case, the word "source," Marian source, Marian origin, has still another, deeper, more immediate meaning.

I'll now make a statement that will be understood by all who are closely associated with Schoenstatt, especially those who can rightly say that their inner development – even more so if it has grown in depth – has always been connected with this place. In all the past important stages of his vocation, the life of our young Federation priest has also been tangibly and verifiably connected with this shrine and hence with the Blessed Mother. Indeed, I may look at our newly ordained priest at the altar as a direct and distinct fruit of grace. How often has this young priest entrusted himself at this place to the protection of the Blessed Mother, to the loving, maternal, and caring protection of the Blessed Mother! Hence we take for granted that the source flowing freely from this place wants to re-absorb the life of this young priest in order to let it permeate the whole world and unfold great fruitfulness.

We are happy about the Blessed Mother's victory. We are happy about the victory of grace bestowed on this young priest from here. Hence: Alleluia! But we are also happy with the young Federation priest because he is the obvious proof, a true image of the interceding omnipotence of the Three Times Admirable Mother. His priestly life should also be Marian because the Blessed Mother wants to protect this unfolding, growing priestly life in an outstanding way in the future as she has done in the past. Under her protection it will be a fruitful life.

We may assume that the priestly life, like every human life, is exposed to great dangers, to the dangers of routine. It is said: *"Quotidiana vilescunt."* Whatever we ordinarily do, will eventually become ordinary. If we handle something every day, in this case the Most Blessed Sacrament, we might easily lose some reverence. But if the Blessed Mother holds her protective hand over this priestly life, we know that she will let him share in her maternal, self-giving joy, in the tender reverence which she felt throughout the historical life of our Lord. She will preserve him from a sense of routine, of everyday routine, from letting it become an ordinary routine. As the Victress who crushes the head of the serpent, she will also protect him from the power and the attacks of the devil. We sense how the devil is alive in the world today, how he frequently celebrates his triumphs today. We also know that the priesthood, in particular, is exposed to the assaults of the devil. Therefore, we rejoice all the more that today a priestly life begins which manifests the Blessed Mother's victory. The One who crushed the head of the serpent once before, will also do so today, will also do so in the future, especially in our own lives because we have placed ourselves entirely under her protection.

Still other battles and difficulties, exterior and interior difficulties, will send shock waves into the life of this young priest. But we know that Our Lady as the protector, as the omnipotent intercessor will always show and demonstrate her profound, maternal gratitude to the young priest as he strives and reaches out for the heights.

With great happiness we sing our alleluia today. After all, the Blessed Mother wants to reveal her glories to the world from here. She did so in our own lives. She often did so in the lives of young priests and she will also do so in the priestly life which begins today in our presence. This fills us with great joy and confidence.

However, the Blessed Mother wants to and also should be the object, the goal of this priestly life, and this makes us especially happy. What unites all of us is the strong common striving to be apostles of the Blessed Mother. We often pray, and we want to give our all "so that the world made new through you pay to your Son his homage due." The world should be renewed through the Blessed Mother. For this reason, we must take the Blessed Mother into the world as the brightly shining light in which the present time should come to see supernatural life once more. This will happen, this must happen. This will and must be the goal of the life of our newly ordained priest too. Therefore we sing: Alleluia! We are happy with the Blessed Mother. We are happy with our young Federation priest. We are also happy with our Mother Thrice Admirable of Schoenstatt.

Indeed, this young priest's life is a Marian priestly life. It is the reason for our joy. But this unfolding priestly life should also be a priestly life dedicated to Schoenstatt. Isn't this also an intense reminder of the gigantic task which Schoenstatt has to fulfill today? We believe that this small spot from where a great spiritual movement spreads into the world, is called to be a pillar of God's Church on earth in this grave hour.

As we are fully aware, God always depends on instruments. This is true of us as well, it is true of Schoenstatt as well. We often pray for instruments that are ready with a joyful and sacrificial spirit to commit themselves to the great mission Schoenstatt has for today: "Send, O Lord, laborers into your vineyard." For us this vineyard is not simply God's Church but also the vineyard of Schoenstatt. "Send, O Lord, laborers into your vineyard." Today God, the Blessed Mother sends us another laborer, a Schoenstatt priest, a priest who sees his life's task in fulfilling and realizing Schoenstatt's mission for today faithfully, joyfully and with a spirit of sacrifice.

Don't you feel how family bonds, how inner bonds of unity between him and us grow stronger? May we not say that he is one of us? He belongs to us, to our family. It is this very sentiment which has driven him, has urged him to celebrate the first most beautiful act of his priestly life, his first holy Mass, here with his family where he grew up, where he did his studies. We want to accompany him to the altar, and quietly and sincerely ask the Triune God that he might draw him into his own inner-Trinitarian divine life. We ask God and the Mother Thrice Admirable that they might accept him as their priest, that they might be near him and support him; that they might see to it that his priestly life will be a richly blessed priestly life in Schoenstatt's spirit.

An ever-growing movement spreads from here into the world. We immediately pause and remember the past. We remember epochs when a major, noteworthy, world-changing religious renewal was initiated by insignificant instruments at some small place. Since we know that such movements were to have and have had a profound influence on the destiny of the Church, we must tell ourselves that we have to actualize both: a movement of the laity and a movement of priests. Another reason for our joy is: God and the Blessed Mother called not only the laity but, also and in a very special way, priests who should continue and complete her work in today's world from here.

And so we rejoice, we are jubilant, we shout the alleluia into today's world which frequently appears so dark and gloomy; we shout it into the heavens and into the heart of the Blessed Mother: Alleluia! At this silent place off the highways and byways of life, we witness today the beginning of a priestly life. It makes us happy and it makes us happier still to know that this priestly life is a Marian priestly life, a priestly life in the spirit of Schoenstatt.

In this spirit, we will now participate in the first holy Mass of this newly ordained priest. We pray and plead that he may experience a renewal of his personal Schoenstatt spirit. We pray for him and he prays for us. He prays that the Blessed Mother will give a far-reaching, victorious mission to all she calls to Schoenstatt, to those belonging to us now and to those who will join us in the future. Then it will one day become true: "that the world made new through you pay to your Son his homage due."

Testimony to the Fruitfulness of Love for Mary

From: J. Kentenich, Talk at the celebration of his silver jubilee of ordination, Schoenstatt, August 11, 1935

There is still someone else I must address. You know the person too – the Mother Thrice Admirable. I think that the whole family should accept the gratitude which has been expressed to me these days and which I have returned to you; that the whole family should direct this very gratitude into the heart of our Mother Thrice Admirable of Schoenstatt.

Years ago, I read about an old and venerable priest who also celebrated his jubilee. As is customary at such celebrations, people collect together everything known about that priest. It was a great deal they had to say about him. At the end of all the words of praise, the priest himself stood up and said: "Yes, you mentioned so many things I was privileged to accomplish. . . " Then he broke out in tears and said: "I owe all this to the Blessed Mother."

I, too, know that numerous people owe a complete transformation of their lives to an encounter with Schoenstatt. I know how many priests state time and time again: What would we be without Schoenstatt! It would be ungrateful to ignore this gratitude. Indeed, I also know and gladly acknowledge that the lives of very few priests have been so exceedingly blessed as mine.

But I also say: Whatever has come into existence, whatever has come into existence through me, whatever has come into existence through you, has come about because of our Mother Thrice Admirable of Schoenstatt.

May I go into detail and tell you what was involved and what forces were at work in the different stages of our growth and development?

First of all, I should like to say that she [the Blessed Mother] has personally formed and molded me from my ninth year on. Generally, I do not like to speak about this, but I think that in this context I may explain it briefly.

Looking back, I have to say that I cannot think of anyone who had a deeper influence on my development. Millions of people break down when they have no one but themselves to depend on as I was. I had to grow up in complete inner solitude because a [new] world had to be born in me, a world which had later to be carried further and passed on. If my soul had come into contact with the cultural trends of that time, if I had been personally attached to someone, I would not be able to say with such certitude today that my education was entirely the work of the Blessed Mother without any other deeper human influence. I realize that I am making quite a statement.

However, you may not think that these are empty phrases because I want to say something gracious about the Blessed Mother. I know that the Blessed Mother has placed her interceding omnipotence and her maternal heart at my service in a singular manner. You have experienced this yourselves and you could check the historical facts: From the moment that she established herself in this shrine, she placed her power and her motherly heart at my disposal for the sake of the work that I was allowed to bring into existence. It is she, too, who gave you to me as my co-workers.

You can explore on your own how everything we see before us today has come into existence because of this deep and simple love for Mary. Hence, am I justified in asking you not to forget her who deserves our special gratitude?

The Priest and the Significance of the Unmarried State

Hail Mary!
For the sake of your purity
keep me pure in body and soul.
Open wide to me your heart
and the heart of your Son!
Give me souls and
keep all else for yourself.

Joseph Kentenich
Prayer from his early childhood.

Regarding the requirement of celibacy for priests, Father Kentenich frankly acknowledged that people's attitude toward celibacy as a form of life has undergone a great change. Hence much of the support which sustained the clergy in the past has eroded. He confirmed that the change in the understanding of human sexuality and the practical consequences have influenced today's thinking. He did not accept any arguments in favor of celibacy for priests which would cast a shadow on Christian marriage and its striving for holiness.

At the same time, it is obvious that he had a high regard for celibacy for the sake of the Kingdom of God. He liked to view celibacy in connection with the evangelical counsels. In many retreats, especially also in retreats for young people, he would speak about the ideal of virginity and make it shine brightly by focusing on the image of the Blessed Virgin Mary. His priestly personality inspired many and influenced them to discern their calling for a virginal lifestyle; communities of the evangelical counsels came into existence in this environment.

His convincing priestly example and his high regard for Christian celibacy and a virginal lifestyle have always been an inspiration and help for many priests to remain faithful to the ideal of priestly celibacy. He was deeply convinced of the inner connection and correlation of the priestly vocation and celibacy as a form of life. In the end, however, he did not count on Canon Law to safeguard celibacy. He saw his task in awakening joy in this ideal; he fostered a living exchange and communion for mutual support and a dynamic striving for apostolic fruitfulness.

A Vanishing Support System

From: J. Kentenich. Fifth talk of the Christmas Convention, Schoenstatt, December 27-30, 1967

To begin with, we know from newspapers and conversations with people that the issue of priestly celibacy is a hotly disputed topic. . . . The reason for this far-reaching interest, I believe, lies largely in the fact that the Council suspended all questions related to this issue. If these questions – as planned – had been openly discussed at the Council, greater calm might reign in the Church. Matters have gone so far that just about any who want to see their names in the press or advertise their literary products will reach their goal most quickly with an attack on celibacy. The topic may well be called a hot potato. It is not even unusual that priests who have been faithful to their vow of celibacy and fully committed to live a celibate life suddenly become confused. They wonder whether everything they had been taught was a mistake. Shouldn't this be corrected today? Haven't we been misled in this and many other related issues?

How may I respond to this statement? Don't expect me to argue in favor of the insoluble connection between the priesthood and celibacy in the western world. Don't get me wrong. Regarding these issues and against the background we are all familiar with, I would say: As far as I am concerned, it is not a foregone conclusion at all that the Holy Spirit might not, after all, stand behind the insoluble bond between the priesthood and celibacy. You can probably gather this from everything we have been discussing. The underlying desire is always to view life from a supernatural perspective, to make ourselves dependent in everything on the Holy Spirit, on the other world and reality. Allow me, therefore, to repeat: When I present these issues like this, don't conclude that I personally take the view: Before long, all this won't be an issue any more at all. Before the Council, it was like this regarding the Index, for example. We did accept it but we knew that sooner or later it would be dropped. It was similar with the use of Latin in the liturgy. It was the law, and we observed it, but we knew that one day this might change.

Hence I am not saying that we should take the view: By tomorrow or the next day, the law will be abolished anyhow. Nowadays it is nothing unusual to hear people talk about "anticipated obedience" – not only regarding this particular issue but in general. I am sure you understand what is meant: One anticipates the expected relaxation [of rules]. Nor do I want to comment on the way dispensations are granted. All these questions are being excluded.

Put positively, the question is: Is it possible for me as a priest who promised celibacy to become a fully integrated person? Or, if I as a person who promised celibacy live a celibate life, can my personality find completion and if so, under what circumstances?

The second statement goes a little deeper and affects our practical everyday life. What we are saying now applies to all who have committed themselves to live a virginal life, who have chosen the virginal state as their state in life. What does this second statement mean? When we observe how life has been changing, how public opinion has been changing, how objective thinking has affected the Church, we realize that the subjective support system has largely disappeared – I am talking about celibacy. In the past, this support system made the decision for us oldies relatively easy or at least easier than it is for the young generation today. What kind of support do I mean? I'll mention three types. The first is the mentality that serving God was necessarily connected with celibacy. For a long time, this had generally been the prevalent view. It might also have made our personal decision much easier. We felt: When my hands touch the Most Blessed Sacrament, it is simply appropriate that I renounce marriage as my state in life. You will understand what is meant. In contrast, modern sexual morality tells us that married life can also be sacred and holy, that marriage and ordained priesthood are definitely compatible and that a married person can also carry out priestly functions.

The second support is similar but highlights a different dimension. According to past thinking, virginity was the highest ethical ideal in Christianity. Hence it was appropriate, in fact it was even deemed necessary that the person who wanted to become a priest had to reach for this highest goal.

May I add a comment? We know that it is even a dogma that the virginal state as a state is more perfect than the state of matrimony. This can easily be misunderstood. Positively seen, this means that the virginal state eliminates many obstacles which make a total self-surrender to God difficult in marriage. By no means does this imply that the virginal person personally is, therefore, more perfect than the married person. In fact, modern thinking even takes the opposite view; namely, that it is more ideal and easier for the married person – presupposing that he or she fulfills the personal mission interiorly and exteriorly within the boundaries of the proper objective rights – to integrate his or her sexuality in a healthy manner than for the unmarried person. Hence, it is a great challenge to the Family Work to see to it that our Schoenstatt couples, our Schoenstatt families, exemplify the ideal of matrimony in an authentic and genuine manner. Without doubt, some constraints will have to be removed from today's mentality.

If we want to go deeper and consider the connection between the married and the celibate person, we simply turn to St. Paul for orientation. He writes to his community in Corinth; that is, not to a single person but to the community as a whole which, after all, consisted primarily though not exclusively of married people. "I betrothed you to Christ to present you as a pure bride to her one husband" (2 Cor 11:2). Do you understand what this means? As virginal persons, we take pride in a *matrimonium spirituale,* a mystic marriage with our

Lord. St. Paul banks on this mystic marriage not only for celibate but also for married people. If you reflect on the rite of matrimony, in fact if you reflect on Pauline teaching on sexuality and family life in general, you will notice that he applies the image of the "head and the members" especially to those who are married. Married people, too, are incorporated into Christ as his members – the man as the head, the woman as the heart.

How does the married person compare to the single person? If we try to understand Pauline teaching a little better, we will have to say: The celibate person enters into only one marriage with Christ, and that is the mystical marriage; whereas the married person enters into a twofold marriage: the mystical marriage with Christ as well as the marriage with a marriage partner who is a reflection, a likeness of God.

I emphasize this in order to draw a closer comparison between the two ideals. If what I am saying is true, isn't it also true that this leads to the disappearance of the support system for us priests?

A third support. In the past, the idea of celibacy meant and took for granted that priests were angels on earth, that they were asexual. This may sound exaggerated, but by and large this was the view people had. Let us not overlook that these ideas, these mistaken and compulsive ideas, have frequently taken a heavy toll on priests who had grown up this way. The suppressed drives later surfaced with great force.

Let us take all this into consideration and gain a clearer view of our personal sexuality; that is, the sexuality which simply belongs to human nature but which is also conquered, controlled, and integrated by the human person.

Reasons for Priestly Celibacy

From: J. Kentenich, Fifth talk of the Christmas Convention, Schoenstatt, December 27-30, 1967

What is the purpose of celibacy, of priestly celibacy that is? When discussing these ideas or when pondering them in order to do some personal soul-searching, we usually refer to the scriptural text: "There are eunuchs who have made themselves eunuchs for the sake of the kingdom of heaven" (Mt 19:12). At issue then is true, genuine celibacy for the sake of the kingdom of heaven. I remain pure, virginal, in order to belong completely and undividedly to God.

Cultural history tells us that the words quoted above are in essence the foundation of monasticism, celibate monasticism. People who want to relate to the modern world in new ways do not want to walk in the footsteps of monasticism. Today's priest does not want that either. He wants to be a *secular* priest; he wants to live in the world and live like the people in the world. Hence, he seeks a new rationale for celibacy connected with his calling. I think I should point this out first lest we come to a rash judgment and do an injustice to those who maintain that they want to serve the world. They want to be prepared to live in the world, not in a monastery. They ask for and want to practice an asceticism appropriate for priests living in the world, not in a monastery.

All in all, what are the reasons for virginity, in general, and for priestly celibacy, in particular?

We differentiate between an ethical motive, a mystical motive, and a sociological motive.

The ethical motive: In our day, the sex drive is often terribly misused. And so, it is appropriate that there are people and classes of people who tell themselves: As a paradigm, we want to live a life of purity to an outstanding degree and, by our example, make people realize that it is possible to control our drives and to channel them correctly. – We might want to ask ourselves whether this motive applies to us.

The mystical motive re-echoes a favorite thought of St. Augustine: Virginity is a *matrimonium spirituale* (a mystical marriage). For a better understanding of this expression, let us recall what we said in the past about the three-dimensional sex drive: *formaliter simplex, virtualiter triplex.* The sex drive includes the physical drive or the drive of the body, the spiritual drive or the drive of the soul, and the creative drive with a desire to form, to give shape and find self-actualization. *Matrimonium spirituale!* In this context, the question arises: How can I as a celibate person – the same applies to the virginal person, in general – master this threefold drive?

To begin with, we think of the physical drive. Actually, we should first examine the drive of the soul, the spiritual dimension, because the drive of one soul to another should be the primary force. This is in essence what it is all about. Nevertheless, talking about the physical drive, what is allowed to a celibate person and what to the married person?

We used to differentiate between three types of purity: instinctive purity, magnanimous purity, and obligatory purity. It goes without saying that the celibate person is obligated to observe the necessary boundary regarding the physical drive. The physical union allowed to the married person as an expression of an innermost spiritual union is not permitted to the celibate person.

However, we do not want to be content with this obligatory physical intactness. There is a higher degree. We used to call it *regula tactus*. It is magnanimous, high-minded purity and intactness according to our state in life. . . .

What is the ultimate and constitutive reason for priestly celibacy? The answer lies in the sociological dimension, meaning that, in Christ and through Christ, the priest is totally committed and dedicated to his spiritual children. It is his willingness to serve. We want to serve souls, we want to serve the Church even to the point of sacrificing our very lives, of pouring out our very blood. Please understand that these reasons apply to all of us. At the moment, the issue is to contemplate the essence of priesthood and from this perspective define the central reason for the virginity, for the celibacy of a priest *living in the world,* because nowadays everything is being questioned. --

By the way, because we attach so much importance to being well acquainted with the objective spirit of the times, I may point out that there is nowadays a great thrust toward serving others, also in non-religious circles. With the sociological motive, we have thus taken up a modern trend and, at the same time, connected it with the essence of priesthood.

The Priest's Life – Not a Solo Flight

I therefore inscribe into your heart
once more with blood and fire
all those I hold so dear
and proceed without fear
along that path in life
which the Father's wisdom
has foreseen for me.

Joseph Kentenich
The Shepherd's Prayer, 1944

As his contacts with priests increased in the twenties and thirties, Father Kentenich time and time again gave fresh impetus to priests, suggesting that priests might get together. Wherever he perceived a desire for greater exchange and togetherness, he encouraged priests to unite in groups and experiment with forming a community of priests. Quite early, he suggested that they study the history of orders and communities of secular priests and search for new forms. Already in the years 1936 and 1937, the founder's suggestions to his confreres led to a draft for a common "rule of life" and a "draft for a constitution for a federation of priests in Queenstown" (cover name for Schoenstatt). From these small beginnings, eventually evolved the various communities of priests within the Schoenstatt Movement.

In 1931, Father Kentenich conducted a retreat with the theme "The mission of priests and the mission of the laity." Already then he tried to open the minds of his confreres for the mission of the laity, which he considered God's will. He believed that only if the laity could be inspired with a strong mission consciousness, would a lay involvement have any staying power and become fruitful.

By observing how Father Kentenich lived his priestly life, many found their own way to combine a degree of personal closeness to people with reverent reserve, and to maintain a warm relationship with many men and women. Reverent, devoted in his love, committed and dedicated to those who entrusted themselves to him, he became an inspiration and model for many priests. How profoundly this ideal of a priestly life formed Father Kentenich is revealed in his address on the occasion of the twenty-fifth anniversary of his priestly ordination. Here we become acquainted with a new way of living in, with, and for one another grounded in priestly fatherliness.

Fostering Greater Community Among Themselves

From: J. Kentenich. Talks for Schoenstatt priests of the Muenster Diocese, January 3, 1966

Let us assume that what we have just discussed is true; namely, that fifty years before the official Church did so, we had been oriented to the Church of the future, to the Church on the newest shore. Furthermore, we have made every effort to anticipate – not only to articulate – what the newest shore will demand of us. If our assumptions are correct, we should understand why, from the beginning, we have considered the idea of community and solidarity among the clergy as extraordinarily important. We might now want to recall everything we wanted to do, everything we attempted to accomplish, everything we taught; but we also want to be grateful. As I see it, we should not take for granted that we have remained a family throughout the past years.

If we carefully consider the idea that his Excellency (Bishop Tenhumberg) has just touched on, I wish to remind you that very early, relatively early, we made an attempt at implementing the suggestion and experiment with a real *vita communis*, to form a community with a common lifestyle. Apparently the time was not ripe for it. I remember what the present Cardinal of Cologne (Frings) said in 1933 on the occasion of participating in a retreat [in Schoenstatt] for the first time, (later he did so for a second time). He said: I don't understand the modern clergy any more at all. We who took our striving seriously were content with the *unio*. But today, the young clergy clamors for community, community. For us, community consisted in that we had common practices which we controlled and had controlled. – This, however, has been our great goal from the beginning. We came into existence at the juncture of the new and the newest times. This means that from a period of extreme individualism, during which I personally had grown up, we entered a period of collectivism. How alone a priest feels today! Yet, this is not even the worst – he has become lonesome and lonely.

Allow me to enumerate three expressions which could indicate the way: being alone, being alone with God, being together. The lonelier we feel in our present-day culture, in our environment, the more we should emphasize being alone with God. However, being alone with God must capture the whole person; that is, it must awaken the social drive. Therefore, a desire for togetherness. We have cultivated a profound togetherness from the beginning. I believe that this is even the secret which might somewhat explain both our ability to exist and our fruitful service.

It seems to me that the need and the desire for deeper togetherness, for some type of community among the clergy, becomes ever more acute. Allow me to use an expression which might sound like a cliché: pluralistic society. If we give it more thought and apply it to practical life, we will understand how difficult it may be in the future for Catholics, for Catholics in general and for us priests in particular, to live in a world, in a secularized world, and to live our calling: to represent God for humanity and to lead humanity to God. . . .

I merely wish to point out this strong desire for deeper community, not for social fellowship. Let me describe how this was. In the course of the years, we have gathered our people around our shrines. What often happened is this: The Rhinelanders liked to be social; the Swabians and the Westphalians were people of inner, spiritual fellowship. It seems, you may well have a mission in this regard, a mission for the whole Schoenstatt Family. Obviously, our mission as priests – aside from Schoenstatt – stands and falls with our ability to overcome our loneliness. I don't want to dwell on it. It is enough just to mention it.

Let me point out that, from the beginning, all forms of community had been the great problem for us. If we tried it at that time and it did not work out, we should examine why it failed. I could probably give an answer. But it has always been our goal and will have to remain so or the family as a whole will not become fruitful.

I think I could now refer to the law of exemplary cases. According to the law of paradigm, there has to be a circle of priests who foster community in an outstanding way. [This is necessary] if the whole family of priests is to become a close-knit spiritual entity, a community which is spiritually bound together – even fused together, as I said this morning when we talked about asceticism – and this on a permanent basis. Our whole mentality must change completely. What the Church has always aimed at is something that lies in the nature of things, in the social structure of the human person and humanity as a whole. According to the law of paradigm, there must always be models that can be emulated. In the future, we will not be able to get along with a great many juridical bonds alone as we did in the past; they won't last. We have to take an undercurrent of the irrational into account today. According to the law of exemplary cases, it is therefore tremendously important that we will succeed in attempting the experiment. The Blessed Mother will guide us in this venture and help us to successfully build up a community of priests who work in the pastoral ministry and live under one roof .

Believing in the Mission of the Laity

From: J. Kentenich. Priesterliche Sendung und Laiensendung, Retreat for priests, Schoenstatt 1931 [The mission of priests and the mission of the laity]

Yesterday we traced our mission consciousness back to the dogmatic reality that we are members incorporated into the God-Man, the Head of the Mystical Body. This leads to the unique awareness of being members [of the Mystical Body of Christ] on the one hand, and of standing alone, on the other. This is our relationship with Christ, but we must also see the role of the members of the Body of Christ, the laity.

The laity, too, has a mission; they, too, are incorporated [into Christ], and Christ wants to fulfill his mission through them also. The mission of the laity is the equivalent of Catholic Action. A strong mission consciousness must be cultivated in the People of God, in the laity, otherwise we will not accomplish anything with all our lay apostolate.

The content and nature of the lay mission.

It is difficult to define the content of this mission; at present we are merely concerned about the source of the mission.

Catholic Action is the God-willed participation of the laity in the apostolate of the hierarchy. God-willed can mean two things: direct or indirect.

We must speak of a direct God-willed participation when we refer to the call which God conveyed through the Church, the Vicar of Christ, the Pope, for the gathering of all Catholic forces. Therefore, the call is willed by God. But this is a superficial interpretation. Those who are knowledgeable would tell us: We are needed now because the Church is in trouble; otherwise nobody has bothered about us. The reason lies deeper. God-willed means that it is directly willed by God. The challenge of the Holy Father was merely the reason to re-emphasize this truth. The lay mission is God-willed just as ours is. However, this divine mission, just like our mission, is dependent on the Church. This might sound a bit blunt, but we want to have dogmatic clarity about the facts.

What is the purpose of Catholic Action? The mobilization of the Catholic inner attitude, the vital forces, and the outer organization. Put differently, the spiritual and organizational mobilization of all Catholic forces. The emphasis is not on the organizational aspect but on the spiritual empowerment.

What did the summons of the Holy Father prepare, cause and implement?

The call to Catholic Action had been prepared by the entire cultural development of the past century. There had been a strong shift in two directions.

People, in general, have more access to political and spiritual-intellectual power. We witness how individual lay men and women slowly emerge and take on responsibilities for the Church. In addition, there is a shift in favor of women to the detriment of men. The emancipation of women has a strong impact. All this furthers Catholic Action.

On the one hand, it is brought about by the great problems of the Church, on the other, through the favorable spiritual conditions. Let us view it from a purely natural perspective. The problems of the Church were brought on by increasing antagonism. Think of the old adversaries: Protestantism, cultural Liberalism; the new adversaries like Nationalism, Socialism, Bolshevism. Here we also witness action, but not in the Catholic sense, and this action has grown immensely. Basically the Church is helpless in dealing with it. The problems of the Church are made worse because a great many Catholics among us are sleeping. It is said that a Bolshevist who explored the conditions in Catholicism came up with the verdict: We do not fear German Catholicism any longer. Two thirds of German Catholicism is dead. – Our forces are not as ready for action as they should be.

Another reason lies in the favorable spiritual conditions in our own ranks. At present strong spiritual trends are alive in the Church: the mystical and the liturgical movements. Naturally, many expectations will remain unfulfilled, but many good and beautiful things are developing. People wake up, a religious sense of responsibility is stirred up. Many lay men and women are concerned and worried about the Church. These factors gave rise to the call for Catholic Action.

Where, however, should we search for the deepest reason?

The mission of the laity is also a pronounced Catholic mission and ultimately goes back to Christ and the mediating responsibility of the Church. We are not used to these expressions, but we must get used to them so that we can go into depths and become knowledgeable.

Mutual Spiritual Connectedness

From: Talk on the occasion of the celebration of the silver jubilee of ordination, Schoenstatt, August 11, 1935

I may and must address a word of thanks to the living. Above all, I am referring to all those who have linked their lives and their destinies for the last twenty-five years, or at least the greater part of these years, with mine. Let me repeat: Try to find another community today which is so much the soul of the soul and the flesh of the flesh of the individual members like our community. Or am I exaggerating? Am I trying, by means of a few diplomatic strokes, to shake off and transfer to others everything that may be unpleasant? No! I am convinced that the entire work which has come into existence is just as much your work as it is mine. I do not know where I should begin. Since the entire celebration has more the character of a family affair, you will not take it amiss if I speak more in the first person than I usually do.

Please listen and examine what I say. Think of all those who bear responsibility for the family – of the oldest and middle generation, of the Schoenstatt Priests, the women, the Sisters of Mary. The great majority (possibly with one exception) have for decades connected their destinies with mine. Am I mistaken when I even state: It can be proven that their calling to Schoenstatt has always been connected with a prior personal encounter. I would be grateful to you if you examined such statements because it is very important to me that we should feel interiorly united with one another in the way the Triune God has intended from all eternity. *"Quod Deus iunxit, homo non separet."* ("What God has joined together, let no one put asunder.")

Our mutual faithfulness will become all the deeper and stronger the more clearly we see how God has mysteriously connected the destinies of people. Where and when did these encounters take place? It would surely be tactless to remove the veil from so many secrets in this public gathering.

When I think of the first generation, of all those who now work directly with me, it is a matter of course that their childlikeness should have found a response in my life and that their entire lives were united with my thinking and willing.

When I think of the first generation of our Schoenstatt priests or of our sisters, I know that in most instances we first got to know one another during a convention or a private conversation. I think I could still prove to each individual person in detail: That is the moment when grace started to work; that is the moment when our mutual contact was made. From this point on our mutual relationship has become exceedingly fruitful. My dear Schoenstatt Family, indeed, this first contact has later always become effective in an original and deep way.

The whole great Work before which we stand today in amazement, has grown out of this united, deep, personal cooperation.

I am sure you will not take it amiss if I make an attempt to describe briefly your share in this work. I must first of all admit that you yourselves have exercised a tremendous influence on my personal development. The words just spoken in jest are true. One of us – one of those who is quite "addicted to attending talks" and would never miss one – relates: When I said that the talks should not be passed on, he answered: 'All he knows, he just has from us.'". . .

The book I read is the book of the times, the book of life, the book of your souls. If you had not opened your souls to me without reservation, most of the spiritual achievements would never have been discovered. One cannot read up on these things in books, one can only read them from life. One of our Sisters of Mary was also right when she said a few days ago: "Because we were so dependent on you, a great deal has been awakened in you that most likely would not have been awakened otherwise." If the first example has more to do with intellectual insight, the second refers to developing the abilities of the heart.

Yesterday evening, one of the older ones among us reminded me that I must already have had a warm heart at the time when they were fighting in the war. I quietly managed to acquire many little things for them, like a balaclava helmet, a warm undervest, etc. Greater and greater warmth for our young people stirred in my heart at that time. This trait has continued to develop in me because of the people God has entrusted to me, and the demands they have made on me.

If you want to know the secret of an almost prodigious fruitfulness, I will tell you the reason lies in a deep, spiritual interconnectedness. Someone has just asked: "What is the source of the riches of your mind and heart?" I may tell you that a person who loves, a person who transfers this love into the heart of God, will to some degree participate in the endless riches of God's love. If there is anything which does not impoverish us, it is love, the gift of the warmth of our hearts. –

All of you who have made demands on me – openly or silently – may [hear me] say: "Without you I personally would not be what I am today." You may not underestimate this point. Again, if you want to know the source of the riches of my mind and heart – now you know it. I hope and pray that God will give all future generations the same opportunities to serve human souls quietly in the background that he has given me. The greatest riches flow back to the person who tries to expend every ounce of strength in the service of souls.

Yet this is still not sufficient. All that I have been allowed to read in your souls always indicated the direction for the particular sub-goals we were striving for. Some day it might be the task for an objective and critical historian to prove that throughout these past twenty-five years, it has always been my main interest to see to it that we consciously pursued our final great goals. Nevertheless, remaining faithful to the particular sub-goals which we had to achieve, discerning these sub-goals and striving to actualize them in an enlightened manner, this, my dear Schoenstatt Family, is absolutely unthinkable without you. And this is where the deeper union of our willing and acting, of our living and loving begins. These things are still so alive in me that in most instances I can tell you: This or that is part of the soul life of this or that person. That is the mysterious source of our deep community spirit. As you know, I usually had no time for social interests. Nevertheless, our loyalty has never wavered, simply because the deep, spiritual connectedness rests on such a solid foundation.

To be a community means that the hearts of the members beat as one. If we may say that the family is marked by a deep community spirit among the members, we must to a great extent attribute it to the fact that most have given their very best to the family. I would like to ask each one of you to admit honestly and humbly what your own life's blood has given to the life of the family. If you do not know, I shall gladly tell you privately.

Should you wish to thank me for anything, it can only be for this: That I have tried to take up what was developing in you, that I have tried to pave the way for you, and once it had come alive to some extent in the community, I have tried to pass it on in the form of a motto. I could tell you who was the main force behind our missionary trend at that time. As the master builder, I worked with individual people, and if I knew that something sound was developing, I withdrew completely, because I expected it to grow.

I could also tell you who the main forces were behind the foundation of the Outer-organization. Keep in mind, it can be proven that it was always in an outstanding way your work, it was your co-operation, it was mainly the result of your efforts that the whole "war organization," the *Congregatio militaris* was carried over to peacetime conditions. This is a classic example: I deliberately did not go to Hoerde because I was absolutely sure of the outcome. Everything had been prepared because every single soul had grown slowly into the whole great Work.

My dear Schoenstatt Family, don't you agree that I am right in joyfully and gratefully redirecting to you the hymns of thanks you have addressed to me? By doing so, I have described in general terms what moves me personally. I could also sing a hymn of praise to those who were not directly included in what has been said. I am thinking now of all those, also of the young generation, who have safeguarded the family by increasing the capital of grace. From the beginning, it has always been my ideal: I will do nothing in the whole family without my co-workers and I know that this thought has permeated all my actions. Even those members with whom I do not have contact act according to the law: "Nothing without us."

Eternity will one day reveal how the smallest and most hidden souls of our family have contributed treasure after treasure. Without their heroic lives of sacrifice and prayer, the family spirit we have today, would be unthinkable. Indeed, nothing without you. I do not know what I should still point out to you.

Imagine, our sisters have existed for ten years without written rules, and yet they have spread out into many spheres of activity. How was it possible? When you look back, you will find that not one iota of the original ideals has been lost. However, our oldest sisters have interiorly so matured over the last ten years that they begin to understand what sort of program we started ten years ago. In the case of the Sisters of Mary, I can prove exactly which spiritual trend came from which sister. Each one can discover herself again and find the best quality of her soul in the family and in everything we are working for. This is an aspect of our education through ideals, our education through organic development and anticipation.

Don't you agree that in this connection I should mention those in particular who work with me up in the retreat house? Without their loyalty I would never have been able to take on so many fields of work. You may want to observe how much life and spirit comes from up there and how each one tries to give his very best for the family.

And so, let me repeat: I should like to capture every hymn of praise you have sung and pass it on to the Triune God, to offer honor to him and thanks to you.

Nor may I forget our young people. This morning, when I gained an insight into the sacrifices they have made, I realized what a heroic youth is emerging. We must become what the old generation represents. Schoenstatt may not develop without us nor without our young generation. I warmly greet our eager and enthusiastic youth, our young women and men.

Our high school boys sent me a letter of congratulations which reflects the spirit of the founding generation: "We want to capture the spirit of the older generation, and with courage and fortitude pass it on to the new generation." [This ideal) is symbolized by the heroes' graves. Our young women are at work as well. Not only the oldest generation but also the youngest should feel included in my gratitude. They, too, are celebrating a bit of the jubilee. It is their jubilee as well.

Openness for New Vocations

Through the most holy mysteries
of our redemption,
send, O Lord,
laborers into your vineyard
and spare your people.

Joseph Kentenich
recommended prayer of petition

The hundredth anniversary of our founder's ordination and the Year of Priesthood announced by our Holy Father are an invitation to keep an eye out for new priestly vocations in our families and communities. Vocations are an entirely free gift from God. And we do have to ask God for this gift, as Father Kentenich often invited and encouraged us to do. We have audio tape recordings of conversations with couples made during his stay in Milwaukee in which he discussed questions concerning vocations.

By means of examples, he showed mothers and fathers how to create an atmosphere in which a vocation can develop in their young children and teenagers. Based on various observations and experiences, he described the conditions and the climate in which a vocation to the priesthood and to other forms of consecrated life can grow.

Priestly Vocation and the Family

From: J. Kentenich. Talk to families, Milwaukee, July 23, 1962

We have to realize how unlikely it is today for someone even to entertain the thought: I could become a priest. These ideas are far too remote. Or, I could become a sister. By and large, we lack the spirit of magnanimity and a desire to conquer the world. We hardly realize how much depends on the parents in this regard. The whole development of the child, also the development of a priestly vocation, is usually influenced by the parents, especially by the mother. When it comes to these very personal things, children usually entrust them to their mothers first. That's why so much depends on a deeply religious atmosphere in the home. Of course, Almighty God is entirely free to bestow his grace for a priestly vocation on anyone.

Generally speaking, when we look into it, we will see that there are four stages in which a vocation to the priesthood or the religious life develops.

The first stage begins relatively early. In fact, I'd say that in a healthy family it is nothing unusual for all children with a religious upbringing to go through that stage. A boy enjoys playing a priest. Look, we may never ridicule such things; we must even encourage a child to do that. This does not indicate by any means that the boy has a priestly vocation. But ordinarily this is the normal stage for a priestly vocation. It is nothing to be ashamed of if we could say in later years: When I was young I thought about it for a while. If a Catholic young girl has a somewhat religious upbringing, it is nothing unusual for her to think: Maybe I will become a Sister, maybe this is something for me. You must understand, such thoughts do not prove a calling.

By the way, let me just add a comment. Nowadays various types of seminars are offered for adult education. The question often arises: What must I do, when should I begin getting ready for parenthood and the education of my children? Some think, as soon as I get married. Others, as soon as I have my first child. The instructor of such a seminar said: No, that's wrong. You must start to educate yourself and prepare for your children at least twenty years before you get married. If you have understood the theoretical thoughts we have just discussed, you will immediately understand that this is true. The ability to educate my children must be my top priority and joy. For twenty years maybe, I don't know for how long, from childhood on, I must educate myself for the sake of my children. [To educate] means to maintain a living contact. If I cannot give life, if I have none to give, how will I be able to educate my children later on? How can I be a "living contact" if I have no life? By the same token, I am tempted to say that if we want to foster priestly or religious vocations in our schools and in our families, we have to start as young children to go the normal way ourselves; at least not put up stumbling blocks. Often enough we are not to blame (if there are no vocations).

The following example might show the importance of little things. A priest was talking about his own vocation to the priesthood. [It began when] he was four years old. His mother was a true Catholic mother who had only one thought on her mind: God has given me children, and I may raise them in order to give them back for the Kingdom of God. Before taking the child to church for the first time, the mother told her child many beautiful things – what it was like (in church), what the priest looked like and that our Lord was in the tabernacle and came on the altar during holy Mass. It was a great experience for the small child when his mother took him to church for holy Mass the first time. He later related: God and the priest were the same in my mind. –

They went to church [and the boy was thinking: I will see God in front of me.] Then the priest entered, a big man with a long cassock. . . . Suddenly the boy became afraid. This is a priest, not God. This is not God. What now? He experienced an inner conflict. But the priest walked over to the boy, shook hands with him and chatted with him. In passing he also said: Listen, son, don't you want to become a priest when you grow up? That was all. But the youngster never forgot it and said: Well, then, it is possible for me to become a priest, isn't it? He always remembered it. It was the beginning of his priestly vocation.

True, it is not ordinarily like that. A priestly vocation goes through many a crisis. In the beginning, it is just like a game, the child acts out holy Mass. I don't know whether this is still done nowadays. Maybe here and there it is still done. Today youngsters probably play engineer. What do they generally play? How to take a car apart. I don't know what else. For the moment we'll stay with the normal way.

Eventually, there comes the time for the second stage. I want to be an altar boy. But being an altar boy is not the main thing. There must also be training and education. If altar boys are not trained and educated, it may well be that becoming a priest is the last thing on their minds because they experienced so many foibles and weaknesses. Yet, this is often the way it happens.

Then the third stage, possibly during the teens with the great crises. Recently I read about Father Lord (US) who used to be in charge of Congregations. He died a few years ago. On one occasion, he talked about his vocation and how it had developed, how he thought of it as a youngster for the first time. These ideas come and no one knows where they come from. Suddenly they are there. Naturally, he went to his mother and said: Mom, I want to become a priest. His mother acted as though she was not interested at all, she just smiled. For him the matter was now closed. Years passed and he never thought of it again. The idea was lost. Until it suddenly returned to him in his teens when his first difficulties arose. His mother acted as though she did not notice anything and let the boy wrestle with it. One day he went to his mother and told her: "Mom, I want to become a Jesuit." Well, answered his mother, now I want to tell you my secret. – What is your secret? – I have prayed every day that God might give you the grace of a vocation. Naturally, *he* was happy and *she* was happy too.

What am I saying? We have to do our part. We may not think it impossible. But naturally, if my ideal is to make as much money as possible, I will transmit this ideal to my son. Naturally, then the children will only think along materialistic lines. Look, if to educate means to maintain a living contact and to awaken life, it goes without saying that I have to possess some degree of spiritual life.

May I briefly repeat the stages a vocation goes through although it does not have to be like that. God has his own ways. Early childhood: the boy plays saying Mass, then he becomes an altar boy; he has to grapple with the crises of his teens; lastly, the vocation matures and the final decision is made.

What did I want to illustrate and tell you? The family is the first seminary of the priest, the most valuable and the most important seminary. Some other time I will explain it in greater detail.

Discerning one's Vocation

From: J. Kentenich. Talk to families, Milwaukee, July 30, 1962

The question has come up: How can a person normally discern whether he or she has a vocation? Let's make it practical. For example, one of your children comes to you and says: I want to become a priest. Well, I have already told you how some mothers reacted. They acted as though they had not heard it or they appeared to be indifferent even though they ardently wished it. And so, let us assume, the child comes and says: I want to become a priest; I want to become a sister. Often enough we lay people settle it by saying: Talk it over with your confessor whether you have a vocation.

What, then, are the criteria for a genuine vocation? There are two views in the Church. People taking the one view believe that a person with a religious calling has to have a constant desire to become a priest or a religious. Unless I have this persistent urge, I have no vocation. The other view is diametrically opposed. I'll come back to that.

At the beginning of this century, about the year 1900, that is between 1896 and 1910, some rather unpleasant church laws were in effect in France. Consequently, priestly vocations dwindled or disappeared altogether. Naturally, it became a matter of controversy: How can one be certain of having a vocation? A book published in

1896 took the view I have just mentioned. A person has to have an extraordinary, clear feeling, a persistent urge to become a priest.

The opposite view stated: First, it is not necessary to have this inner urge and second, this feeling is not a definite proof that a person has a vocation. To gain some certainty whether someone has a priestly calling – naturally, the same applies to a religious vocation – it is enough to know that first, a person has the good intention to become a priest or religious and second, that the necessary requirements can be met. In a moment I'll come back to details.

Of course, this led to an intense conflict among theologians. In the end, the controversial matter was taken to Rome. From 1904 on, Pius X was pope. He appointed a committee to study the question. The pope then approved the findings of the committee. Since then we know the criteria which help a person to discern a priestly vocation.

This does not mean that I *must* pursue this priestly calling. I *may* become a priest if the following conditions are met. What are the particular conditions?

First, the necessary physical health for fulfilling the priestly vocation; second, the necessary spiritual health; third, the necessary intellectual abilities because being a priest demands a certain degree of knowledge. So then, these requirements must be met to become a priest. These are down-to-earth considerations.

Religious requirements must necessarily be met as well: I must have a religious bent, take joy in religious matters; it does not have to be a tangible joy, just a religious mind-set, an interest in the Kingdom of God, love for the Church and, lastly of course, I must be able to meet the ethical demands, that is, live a virginal life because – at least in the western Church – the priesthood is bound up with celibacy. These are simple down-to-earth questions.

Hence, I must be able to meet these conditions, I must have the ability to fulfill these conditions; secondly, I must have the intention of becoming a priest. If all these elements are present, I may assume that I have an inner calling for this or that state in life.

But I am not under the *obligation* to choose this vocation. In addition, there is also an exterior call; namely, a bishop must accept me or, in the case if a religious vocation, a community must accept me. You see, actually the demands are quite simple.

Bibliography

The Expectations a Priest Faces

Confronted with Contradictory Expectations
J. Kentenich, Ich will ihm Vater, er soll mir Sohn sein [I will be a father to him, he shall be my son]. Sermon at a newly ordained priest's first holy Mass with the German Congregation at St. Michael's Church, Milwaukee, February 7, 1965, in: Father Joseph Kentenich, Aus den Menschen – fuer die Menschen, Vallendar-Schoenstatt 1970, Patris Verlag, pp. 103-105 [Chosen from among the people – for the people]

Challenged by the Dynamics of the Times
J. Kentenich, Die moderne priesterliche Werktagsheiligkeit, Retreat "Priesternot," Schoenstatt July 23-29, 1939, rev. ed. 2007-08, pp. 128-129 [Everyday sanctity for the modern priest]

Balancing Dedication to Others and Preserving his Own Identity
J. Kentenich. Die moderne priesterliche Werktagsheiligkeit, Retreat "Priesternot," Schoenstatt July 23-29, 1939, rev. ed. 2007-08, pp. 121-122 [Everyday sanctity for the modern priest]

The Priest – a Man of God and a Builder of Bridges

Called by God – Consecrated to God – Sent by God
J. Kentenich, Retreat for the Bethlehem Fathers, Immensee, Switzerland, Introductory talk, August 29, 1937, in: Joseph Kentenich., Retreat for priests, Vallendar-Schoenstatt 1979, Patris Verlag, pp. 22-24. 27-28 [Childlikeness before God, p. 4 ff., trs. by Fr. Jonathan Niehaus]

177

Chosen from Among the People – for the People

J. Kentenich, Aus den Menschen – fuer die Menschen Sermon at a newly ordained priest's first holy Mass with the German Congregation at St. Michael's Church, Milwaukee, November 3, 1963, in: Father Joseph Kentenich, Aus den Menschen – fuer die Menschen. Sermons about the priesthood, Vallendar-Schoenstatt 1970, Patris Verlag, pp. 49-54 [Chosen from among the people – for the people]

Participation in the Priesthood of Christ

Christ – the One Priest

J. Kentenich, Die moderne priesterliche Werktagsheiligkeit, Retreat "Priesternot," Schoenstatt July 23-29, 1939, rev. ed. 2007-08, pp. 67-69 [Everyday sanctity for the modern priest]

Fruitful Participation in the Priesthood of Christ

J. Kentenich, Marianische Werkzeugsfroemmigkeit, Vallendar-Schoenstatt 1974, Schoenstatt Verlag, pp. 200-205 [Marian Instrument Piety, trs. by Fr. W. Brell, rev.]

Original Priestly Striving for Holiness

J. Kentenich, Die moderne priesterliche Werktagsheiligkeit, Retreat "Priesternot," Schoenstatt, July 23-29, 1939, rev. ed. 2007-08, pp. 95-97 [Everyday sanctity for the modern priest].

A Profoundly Prophetic Task

The Prophetic Priest

J. Kentenich, Brief 1958, in: Das Priesterbild des Verbandes, unedited, typed manuscript published by the Schoenstatt Institute of Diocesan priests, pp. 69-70 [The image of a priest of the Schoenstatt Priests' Institute]

The Priest and his Belief in Divine Providence
*J. Kentenich, Retreat for priests in the Marienau, Schoenstatt 1951,
unedited, pp. 117-119*

A Messenger of Grace
*J. Kentenich, Sermon at the first holy Mass of Fathers Bezler,
Fischer, and Mutzenbach, Schoenstatt July 4, 1929, unedited, typed
manuscript published by the Secular Institute of the Schoenstatt
Sisters of Mary, pp. 10-13*

Orientation to the Good Shepherd

Jesus – a Shepherd's Love and a Shepherd's Care
*J. Kentenich, Eighth talk in: USA Tertianship, Mount Sion 1988,
unedited, pp. 177-183*

Combining Fatherly and Motherly Service like St. Paul
*J. Kentenich, Krise um Regierungsformen, [Crisis regarding forms
of government] Milwaukee, September 1961, in: Autoritaet und
Freiheit in schoepferischer Spannung, edited by Herta Schlosser,
Vallendar 1993, Schoenstatt Verlag, pp. 93-95 [Authority and
freedom in creative polarity]*

Creating a Spiritual Home for Those Entrusted to him
*J. Kentenich, Kampf um die wahre Freiheit, Retreat for priests,
Schoenstatt, January 7-10, 1946, unedited, pp. 240-244
[The struggle for true freedom]*

Challenged to Live Apostolic Holiness

The Ideal of Apostolic Holiness
*J. Kentenich, Die moderne priesterliche Werktagsheiligkeit, Retreat
"Priesternot," Schoenstatt July 23-29, 1939, rev. ed. 2007-08, pp.
63-64 [Everyday Sanctity for the modern priest]*

Becoming a Golden Priest

J. Kentenich, Retreat for Schoenstatt Fathers, Schoenstatt November 1-8, 1966, Tenth talk, November 7, 1966, in: Father Joseph Kentenich to his Pars motrix, vol. 5, Schoenstatt, 2nd ed. 1990, pp. 257-261

Living as Vessels of the Spirit

J. Kentenich, Seelenfuehrer Kurs Mystik, Schoenstatt, August 30 - September 3, 1927, unedited, pp. 1-3 [Retreat about pastoral ministry, mysticism]

The Priest and the Blessed Mother

Our Method is Marian

J. Kentenich, Priesterliche Sendung und Laiensendung. Retreat for priests, Schoenstatt October 11-18, 1931, unedited, typewritten manuscript published by the community of Schoenstatt Priests, 55 pages, pp. 46-47 [The mission of priests and the mission of the laity]

The Marian Priest

J. Kentenich, Der marianische Priester, Retreat for priests, Schoenstatt 1941, unedited, typewritten manuscript published by the Schoenstatt Institute of Diocesan Priests, Simmern 1993, pp. 3-4 [The Marian priest]

The Beginning of a Marian Priestly Life

J. Kentenich, Sermon at a newly ordained priest's first holy Mass, Schoenstatt, Easter 1934, unedited, typewritten manuscript published by the Secular Institute of the Schoenstatt Sisters of Mary, 30 pages, pp. 24-28

Testimony to the Fruitfulness of Love for Mary

J. Kentenich, Talk at the celebration of his silver jubilee of ordination, Schoenstatt August 11, 1935, unedited, typewritten manuscript published by the Secular Institute of the Schoenstatt Sisters of Mary, pp. 19-20

The Priest and the Significance of the Unmarried State

A Vanishing Support System
J. Kentenich, Fifth talk in: Christmas Convention 1967, Talks by the founder of the Schoenstatt Family, Father Joseph Kentenich, typewritten manuscript published by the Secular Institute of the Schoenstatt Sisters of Mary, Vallendar-Schoenstatt, pp. 103-109

Reasons for Priestly Celibacy
J. Kentenich, Fifth talk in: Christmas Convention 1967, Talks by the founder of the Schoenstatt Family, Father Joseph Kentenich, typewritten manuscript published by the Secular Institute of the Schoenstatt Sisters of Mary, Vallendar-Schoenstatt, pp. 112-121

A Priest's Life – Not a Solo Flight

Fostering Community Among Themselves
J. Kentenich, Third talk for Schoenstatt Priests of the Muenster Diocese, Muenster January 3, 1966, in: J. Kentenich, Propheta locutus est, vol. 3, pp. 91-95

Believing in the Mission of the Laity
J. Kentenich, Priesterliche Sendung und Laiensendung, Retreat for priests, Schoenstatt 1931, unedited, typewritten manuscript published by the community of Schoenstatt Priests, 55 pages, pp. 16-17 [The mission of priests and the mission of the laity]

Mutual Spiritual Connectedness
J. Kentenich, Talk at the celebration of his silver jubilee of ordination, Schoenstatt August 11, 1935, unedited, typewritten

manuscript published by the Secular Institute of the Schoenstatt Sisters of Mary, pp. 9-17

Openness for New Vocations

Priestly Calling and the Family
J. Kentenich, Talk for families, Milwaukee, July 23, 1962, unedited, to be published as part of the series: Father Joseph Kentenich, On Monday Evenings. Speaking to Families, Schoenstatt Verlag

Discerning One's Vocation
J. Kentenich, Talk to Families, Milwaukee, July 30, 1962, unedited, to be published as part of the series: Father Joseph Kentenich, On Monday Evenings. Speaking to Families, Schoenstatt Verlag

Book cover

Background image:
Vine motif on the rock well in the Priester- and Bildungshaus Mount Moriah, Schoenstatt. Design and execution: Walter Schmitt. Photography: Oskar Buehler